OLD
SAYBROOK

Aerial view of Main Street. *Image courtesy of Old Saybrook Historical Society.*

OLD SAYBROOK

A Main Street History

———————

TEDD LEVY

Foreword by Barbara J. Maynard

THE
History
PRESS

Published by The History Press
Charleston, SC
www.historypress.com

Copyright © 2020 by Tedd Levy
All rights reserved

Front cover images: (top left) courtesy of Sally Perrenten, (top right) courtesy of Sally Perrenten, (lower left) courtesy of Old Saybrook Historical Society and (lower right) courtesy of Old Saybrook Historical Society. Back cover images: (top) courtesy Chamber of Commerce, (bottom) courtesy of Old Saybrook Historical Society.

First published 2020

Manufactured in the United States

ISBN 9781467143417

Library of Congress Control Number: 2020934365

Dedicated to those who act to improve their communities.

CONTENTS

Foreword, by Barbara J. Maynard   9
Acknowledgements   17
Introduction   19

1. A Quick Trip on Main Street   23
2. "Narrowville" with the Waybackers   60
3. Village of Elms   66
4. The Lines at the Junction   69
5. Writers and Fighters at the Upper Cemetery   73
6. Saybrook's Monkey Farm   76
7. Remembering the Sacrifice   79
8. Merchants Organize   82
9. A Place Called Saybrook Home   88
10. Past Posts   92
11. Muskets on Main   96
12. Ladies of the Club   101
13. The Value of Penny Candy   105
14. Music and Drama on Main   109
15. Street "Pedalers"   113
16. Spare Time   116
17. Matinee on Main   120
18. Keeping the Faith   124
19. Planting Seeds   127

Contents

20. From Factory to Main Street   131
21. When We Were a Couple o' Kids   135
22. Teammates Start the Fire Department   139
23. Skills and Drills at Seabury Institute   143
24. Leaving a Legacy   147
25. The Hart of the Town   151

Bibliography   155
About the Author   157

MEMORIES OF MAIN STREET

By Barbara J. Maynard

Barbara J. Maynard has had a love affair with Old Saybrook since she was four years old, pulling clams from the mud at Saybrook Manor. For twenty years, she and her husband, George, owned and operated the Saybrook Hardware Store, and from 1973 to 1989, she served as Old Saybrook's selectwoman. Both before and after her time in office, Barbara has been a leading promoter of the town and its history. This essay contains reflections on some of her Main Street experiences over the years.

———————

Small New England towns seem to have certain feelings about them. Old Saybrook's history indicates that, since 1635, when the first fort builders landed at the mouth of the Connecticut River, the town experienced hardships we cannot imagine. Early records indicate that every day was filled with fear, anxiety and loneliness. As the early settlement grew, pathways became roads. A road to the cornfield was needed, and a cart path heading north along the river eventually became today's beautiful, wide Main Street. As new people arrived, and the shipping industry grew at Saybrook Point, homes, barns and small stores were built. Main Street was the logical location for the expansion of the town. A government was formed, a militia kept the peace and selectmen governed.

This aerial view shows Main Street and its relationship to the surrounding environment, including the Connecticut River and Long Island Sound. *Photograph courtesy of Kasey Commander.*

For many years, Main Street was the only route through Old Saybrook. The Boston Post Road led travelers to Main Street and then took them west, to the Oyster River District and Westbrook. Local stores along Main Street provided the town's early residents with simple necessities; some were locally produced, and others were eventually imported. The small stores along Main Street thrived; the wide gravel roadway became part of Route 154, and it was maintained by the state's department of transportation. Solid surfaces on local roads were tarred and sanded, so getting stuck in the mud was a thing of the past.

Since the 1600s, Main Street has been the heart of Old Saybrook. All of the town's services are on Main Street—ambulance, fire department, town hall and police department. Three of the town's early churches are on Main Street. For many years, there was also a doctor's office there. The post office has had many homes on Main Street. The chamber of commerce now greets citizens at the head of Main Street. The first town hall was built as a theater, with offices and a jail cell on the lower level. The hallway on the lower level also served as a local courtroom with a local judge. If a resident was arrested and went to the local court, everyone in town knew about it and was either entertained or embarrassed. Crime was not a serious problem in

Old Saybrook. Today's town hall was the original "new" brick consolidated school, and it was built in 1937. The first consolidated school, a wooden three-story structure, replaced three district schools: one at the Ferry, one in the Saybrook Point area and one on Schoolhouse Road that served the Oyster River District.

Prior to the 1938 hurricane, Main Street was lined with the town's centennial elm trees. All of the towns in Connecticut were offered elm trees in 1876 to commemorate the centennial of the signing of the Declaration of Independence. Old Saybrook received fifty-six trees, one for each signer. On July 4, 1876, a town meeting was held, and a motion was made that two citizens from each school district be appointed to plant the fifty-six trees. There are still five centennial elm trees that can be identified in town. They are now known as the survivor trees. Many young seedlings from the surviving trees are now growing in safe places, and they are hopefully resistant to Dutch elm disease. The loss of the Main Street elms in 1938 brought feelings of lasting sadness to Old Saybrook's residents.

Main Street has experienced floods, several hurricanes, serious fires and accidents. It has been widened to accommodate the town's need for parking. It's been dug up for drainage systems and underground wires. Main Street was closed to all traffic (it is a state road) when Governor Ella Grasso closed down all of Connecticut's roads during a whopper of a snowstorm that hit the state in the 1980s. Main Street has recovered from most of its problems and is now dressed up for different seasons. Local volunteer organizations purchase and fly flags, and the islands are turned into summer gardens, planted with hundreds of annuals by dozens of dedicated Garden Club members. Starting on Thanksgiving, the gas light lamp poles are decorated with lighted evergreen wreaths and large red bows. Residents and visitors look forward to the seasonal decorations.

Main Street seems to reflect the feelings of Old Saybrook residents. Over the years, deaths, tragic illnesses, accidents and numerous wars have brought much sadness to the town's residents. Deaths of family members and friends brought visitors to the homes of the bereaved. Visitors offered food, flowers, wood and help with chores, snow shoveling and children. Older residents have said that the town was a big family.

When Franklin Roosevelt died in 1945, I was coming out of a store on Main Street when I noticed that cars were suddenly stopping. I saw one woman get out of her car and shout very loudly, "President Roosevelt just died!" Main Street knew. People gathered around radios in stores and restaurants and spoke in quiet voices. They asked, "What will happen now?" Concerns were discussed, and residents were glued to their radios. A feeling of loss and sadness was felt on Main Street and beyond. Flags were flown at half-mast, and churches were opened. Older residents, who had President Roosevelt to thank for social security, were especially upset. Main Street mourned.

A great sadness also came to Main Street the day that President John Kennedy was shot in Texas. I was taking a school census for the board of education to help determine the number of students that would be in Old Saybrook's schools in the upcoming years. Dr. Dan Terray was answering my questions when, suddenly, his wife came to the door and sobbed, "Someone just shot our president." Main Street changed instantly; townspeople were crying and holding each other, churches opened again, people spoke in quiet voices and all of the flags were lowered. Old Saybrook mourned from Main Street to the back roads.

My son, Barry, recalls getting on the school bus, where he was met by his favorite bus driver at the door. The driver asked all of the students to sit down and be very quiet; she then turned the radio on, and the students learned of the tragedy. Barry still remembers that it was a very quiet ride. Parents who had just heard the news went to the bus stops to meet their children. Main Street mourned again, and the shock, sadness, disbelief and anger lasted for several days.

THE EFFECT OF WARS ON MAIN STREET

Even though Old Saybrook had a small population during World War I, a number of the town's men fought in the war. They were local farmers, fishermen, shopkeepers, carpenters and masons. The town's women knitted socks and hats and went to work where they could help to keep their families fed and clothed. A list of the town's World War I veterans was etched on a monument on Main Street and is on the town green today. Many families of these veterans still live in Old Saybrook.

The memories of World War II are very real to me. I was a high school student at the Main Street School. In 1944, there were twenty girls and four boys in our graduating class. Many of our boys joined up; some even joined before they met the required age. Our graduation was subdued. Prayers were said and patriotic songs were sung by the high school glee club. We had a sparse group for our senior prom; the parents and school administrators helped fill the space in the decorated gymnasium. I'm sure many can remember where they were on Sunday, December 7, 1941, when Japan attacked Pearl Harbor. My boyfriend and, now, husband of more than seventy years, George, and I were at my home near the beach at Saybrook Manor. There, we heard the words of President Franklin Roosevelt: "A date which will live in infamy." Many young men and some women joined the service as soon as they could get to the recruiting office in New Haven.

Main Street, especially near the post office, was the place to gather, hear the latest news and share newly received censored letters from the town's men and women from all over the world. Dreaded news came by telegraph. The telegraph office was at the head of Main Street, near the site of today's Saybrook Home. When a wire came to inform a local family that someone had been killed in action or was missing in action, within a short time, the town would know of the tragedy. Hearts were broken, tears flowed and flags were lowered. Churches held special prayer services. The clergy seemed to be everywhere, trying to comfort families. Main Street businesses hung black ribbons on signs, and the town hall had black ribbons on its tall white columns. Main Street had a sense of sadness and fear. It was quiet.

During World War II, Old Saybrook's population was about 2,500 in the winter. When Europe and England were bombed, there was a critical need for all kinds of supplies. Many small local industries were started in Old Saybrook to support the war effort. Gliders were built in Deep River, and the crates that were used to ship them were built in Old Saybrook. The small factory was located at the current site of McDonald's. Locally manufactured war supplies were shipped to ports in Boston from the Old Saybrook Railroad Station.

Local residents were recruited as airplane spotters. They had the responsibility of identifying the planes that flew over the town and the directions in which they were traveling. The area on top of the Main Street School, now the town hall, was constantly manned by spotters. Residents along the shoreline had to have blackout shades, and they were required to paint the top half of their headlights black. Streetlights were turned off along the shore, as the danger of German subs in Long Island Sound was very real.

Main Street stores served the town's residents as well as they could. Ration stamps were used for sugar, meat, butter and other goods. Local residents grew victory gardens and raised chicks and ducks. There was a lot of trading and sharing going on. Homemade "hootch" was even available—it was probably a much-needed necessity.

STORMS AND FLOODS

Main Street has seen it all; elm trees have crisscrossed over the street, and it was flooded to the steps of the town hall during the 1938 hurricane. Many hurricanes have hit along Old Saybrook's vulnerable seventeen miles of coastline, causing a lot of damage. The flood in 1982 actually lifted the pavement on the town's roads. Thirteen inches of rain fell in just two hours, and it caused the town to be without power for many days. It was a real hardship, as candles were hard to come by. The snowstorms also caused walking and parking problems along Main Street, where piles of snow gathered.

1970s AND 1980s

During the 1970s and 1980s, Old Saybrook had a lot to celebrate. In 1976, Old Saybrook celebrated the nation's bicentennial. Parades were held, and floats that depicted the town's history were created by the neighborhoods. There was a Lion Gardiner in full armor and Mohegan natives in full feathers, shell beads and leather outfits. An ox cart pulled by well-controlled oxen moved slowly down Main Street. A replica of the town's outer light was created by clever carpenters, and it was just able to fit under some street wires. Many ladies made costumes that resembled those that would have been worn in the town throughout the preceding centuries. Kids had old-fashioned toys, like handmade wagons, hoops and drums. Many of their costumes were made from feed bags, as they would have been in the old days.

Main Street loves a parade. In 1985, the Saybrook Colony celebrated its 350th anniversary with a celebration that lasted throughout the entire year. All of the towns that were a part of the original colony participated, and the historical societies in all of our towns were very busy!

On July 4, 1976, a grand ball was held in Old Saybrook's largest space: the gym at the junior high school. Kathleen Goodwin and Merle Patrick were the grand marshals of the ball. Approximately two hundred residents in costume attended, and at midnight, an original cannon was fired—that was more spectacular than a birthday cake with two hundred candles! Main Street celebrated; all of the flags in town—some with thirteen stars—were on display on houses, flagpoles and even cars.

Each year, Main Street hosts a Memorial Day Parade, an event that started in the early 1900s. Hundreds of residents march in the parade, representing their local organizations. During every Christmas season since 1971, hundreds of people have lined Main Street for the Torchlight Parade. Fife and drum corps march in formation, playing appropriate music. It is wonderful and could only happen on Main Street.

TOWN HALL AND VISITORS

Each year, the town hall's employees welcomed students from the Main Street School to their offices. The students were shown how everything worked—how the money came into the tax office, went to the treasurer and then went to the bank. They were told how that income covered the bills for their education. As they toured the original 1911 town hall, from the attic to the lower floor, they seemed to be most interested in the old jail cell. Many letters said that "the jail was neat" and that the cookies were good, too.

I served as the first selectwoman for sixteen years. I met the kindergarten class of 1973 and watched them graduate twelve years later. It was such a pleasure to watch them grow from cub scouts, to little-league ballplayers, to members of the band and glee club and, finally, to college students. Many of the town's students took part in the activities on Main Street.

I know that Main Street has made it through all these years and that it will make it through many, many more. Our Main Street is forever. Our town is a great place to live, because it has a special place called Main Street.

ACKNOWLEDGEMENTS

Several people have helped ease my way in preparing this publication, and they deserve recognition and my grateful appreciation for their help. I would like to send a special thank-you to Barbara and George Maynard for their willingness to share their knowledge and memories and for their unwavering support of Old Saybrook and its history. My thanks also go to Roy Lindgren for being a reliable source of difficult-to-obtain images of Old Saybrook and for his willingness to share the stories that go with them.

I would also like to thank several generous and supportive colleagues, including Sally Perreten, who happily shared her many engaging Main Street photos; J.T. Dunn, who allowed the use of his essay on the beginnings of the Old Saybrook Fire Department; Sue Braden, editor of the *Shoreline Times*, who encouraged and published earlier versions of these essays; Bob Czepiel, who permitted the use of his dramatic photographs; Kasey Commander, who readily shared many distinctive photos; and Christine Nelson, Old Saybrook town planner, who provided many valuable ideas and useful materials.

I also gratefully appreciate the assistance, patience and expertise I received from the friendly volunteers at the Old Saybrook Historical Society Archives, including Kerry Auld, Margaret "Bucky" Bock, Diane Hoyt, Teddi Kopcha, Diane Lyons, Greg Thompson, Marie Vasile and, for her dedication and inspiration, Old Saybrook Historical Society president Marie McFarlin.

And, for her steadfast support, I would like to thank my wife, Carol.

MAIN STREET IN OLD SAYBROOK

*T*here's an old familiar tune that says, "I have often walked down this street before," and if you're looking for a good place to sing that refrain, look no further than Main Street in Old Saybrook. For many towns in America, there is no street like Main Street. Streets help shape our lives, and some serve as shorthand when describing our character—easy street, dead end, side street—and some, like Wall Street, serve to describe an entire class. Main Street represents ordinary people and traditional values; it's a place to socialize, to watch a parade or to make a purchase in a mom-and-pop shop. In song and legend, Main Street is the heart and soul of small-town America.

For years, Saybrook was noted for its wide Main Street shaded by great arching elms. A visitor in 1902 noted that "the village, the evening [he] arrived was, to my eyes, quite entrancing....In the mild May twilight, I walked from end to end of the long main street. The birds were singing, and from the seaward marshes came the piping of the frogs and the purring monotone of the toads; lines of great elms and sugar maples shadowed the walks." A few years later, in 1907, another described the town as "one of the most picturesque towns in New England....[It] has an entrancing charm for the tourist and summer visitor." He, too, noted that "the wide main street is shaded by long lines of great elms and sugar maples, and the substantial houses give a delightful sense of repose and comfort."

Main Street, however, was not always *the* main street in Saybrook. In the town's earlier days, the major thoroughfare was Water Street, now

North Cove; it was the home of sailing ships and coastal trade, bustling with wharfs, taverns and shops. Robert Burns and Frank Young recognized that commerce was changing, so they moved their North Cove store to the new center of town, where they sold candy, tobacco, clothes, pots, pans and general merchandise. Robert lived nearby in an octagonal house that was constructed by Horace Archer; it was supposedly built with plans and materials that were ordered from Sears and Roebuck.

As technology, trade and industry changed, economic activity moved to the wide main street of impressive homes of prominent residents. And by the early 1900s, this stretch of mostly open land sported a grammar school and a new town hall. The new town hall even had a jail in the basement, where the local constable could offer overnight accommodations for the town drunk or, as they did in later years, provide temporary lodging for those in need or for transients who were searching for work. Small businesses opened that were owned, operated and patronized by local residents. Local customers, as well as those from other towns, found that travel was easy on the trolley system that connected the shoreline communities. A town pump at the corner of Main and West Main Streets, now the Old Boston Post Road, provided water for thirsty residents and the remaining horses. Luxurious steamboats brought visitors to the steamboat dock at Saybrook Point, and the railroad connected the town with New Haven and New London. There was also a direct route from Hartford to the station at Saybrook Point, with a spur across the cove to Fenwick.

On the eve of the Great Depression, the town had a population of approximately 1,400 people and perhaps a dozen stores. A general store run by the Stokes Brothers provided the town's residents with a variety of groceries and goods that were delivered directly to residents' homes in a Ford truck. The store was also the place for picking up mail, and the office of Dr. Wolfe, the only dentist in town, was upstairs. For many years, it was the social center of the community, as men sat around on pickle barrels bragging, complaining and talking about whatever men talk about when there's nothing much else to do. The scene was memorialized in a February 1909 *New York Herald* poem titled "In Stokes Grocery Store," which was written by Saybrook author and humorist Joe Cone*:

A circle gathers every night,
Say twenty-odd, or more,
Around the big, invitin' stove
In Stokes grocery store.

Here's where the farmin's carried on,
Here's where the hay is raised,
Here's where the cords uv wood are cut,
An' where the stock is grazed.
Here's where the monstrous clams are dug
Instead un 'long the shore,
Great deeds are done around the stove
In Stokes grocery store.

Next door was the Gilt Edge restaurant, which was widely described as a "greasy spoon"; it even had a pool hall. Nearby was the Economy Market, which later became Merle Patrick's Country Store, and Tinner Smith's Stove Shop, today Esty's Lamp Store. Outside, a set of cranked gasoline pumps were owned and operated by justice of the peace Tom Kerwin. Farther north on Main, Albert "Dud" Dudley constructed a building in 1928 that included, then and now, Saybrook Hardware, along with a lawn mower shop, a flower shop, a beauty salon and Dan Adanti's Bar and Grill. It later housed the town's first radio and television store, a five-and-ten-cent store, Watson's Drug store and the A&P Market.

Commercial development took a large step forward in the early 1930s, when Frank Palmer of Hartford and W.W. Rochette, a Saybrook contractor, bought land on the corner of Sheffield and Main Streets and constructed a commercial building that held a supermarket, a print shop, a restaurant, a corner drugstore and, behind it on Sheffield Street, a barbershop. The corner was located near the school, and it was a popular stopping place for generations of students who nursed milkshakes and ogled the opposite sex at Ranelli's Rexall Drug Store.

The town's first movie theater opened in 1937, and it could seat six hundred patrons. Alongside it was the post office, Young's Soda Shop and Fred's Beauty Shop. Close by was a popular bowling alley that served as a gathering place, and it was busy with individual and league play. Next door, Joe Snead provided reliably good food at Joe's Diner, which is now the location of Penny Lane Pub.

Time marches on. Until the pandemic in 2020, socializing moved into restaurants. Many of the large houses of prominent residents have been converted to businesses and some have been demolished and are gone forever—others are threatened with this same fate. The large, universally admired elms were destroyed by the 1938 hurricane and Dutch elm disease, and other long-standing trees have been damaged, removed and often not replaced. Green lawns have become black asphalt, as parking has become more important than parks. It's changed, but there's still a good reason for residents to sing out, "Let the time go by, I won't care if I can be here on the street where you live."

*Joe Cone (1869–1918) was a musician, artist, poet, printer and humorist. His early years were spent in the Moodus and Haddam Neck area. Among his many achievements was heading the group that established a theater, which later became the town hall and is, today, the Katharine Hepburn Cultural Arts Center.

I

A QUICK TRIP ON MAIN STREET

*O*ld Saybrook's Main Street runs in a flat, straight north–south line for about two miles, and then, at some little-known point near North Cove Road, it becomes College Street. It then continues for less than a mile to Saybrook Point and Long Island Sound. The business area includes a mix of small commercial buildings, converted older houses, the post office, a theater, churches, the town hall, a fire station, restaurants and private residences, and as it continues south, it becomes entirely residential until it reaches Saybrook Point.

Main Street's wide, divided lanes and diagonal parking characterize its business section and make it easy for residents and visitors to either travel though or stop and shop. Parades, antique shows, arts and crafts events, educational and informational activities, musical performances and promotional events are typically held along Main Street. The street's geographic location within the town, its design and development and its mix of essential services and desirable goods, combined with a continual effort by concerned and active merchants, public officials and residents, makes Main Street the core of the Old Saybrook community.

Much of the information that follows is updated from Old Saybrook walking tour brochures; the most recent one was developed in 1993 by Laurence Reney and Elaine Staplins. To be sure, every place on Main Street has a history, but regrettably, only a few of those stories can be told here. So, start here, on these pages, and finish your journey on the street.

North Main Street

Railroad Station

In 1855, land was sold to the New Haven and New London R.R. Company, and a depot was erected by the New York, New Haven and Hartford Railroad Company and the Connecticut Valley Railroad Company. The current station was constructed in 1873, and it was divided into ladies' and gentlemen's waiting rooms, a telegraph and ticket office, a ladies' dressing room, a lunch counter and a dining room with a kitchen attached and baggage room. The eastern section was angled away from the western section, with tracks that ran south, to Saybrook Point, to accommodate the residents of Fenwick. The building was extensively upgraded in 2019–2020.

North Main Street

Upper Cemetery

While the sign at the Upper Cemetery states that it was founded in 1750, its first burial did not occur until 1787. The 2.7-acre cemetery is the final resting place for many prominent Saybrook families, including the Bushnells, the Whittleseys, the Clarkes, the Chalkers and the Spencers, as well as Thomas Acton (1823–1898), a New York City politician and reformer and an Old Saybrook summer resident for whom the library is named. Here, too, is Fero, "the faithful slave" of William Lynde. The cemetery holds forty-eight identified veterans from the French and Indian War, the American Revolution, the War of 1812 and the Civil War.

15 North Main Street

Edward Sanford House

Built around 1815, this house was the birthplace of Maria Sanford (1836–1920), a noted American educator and a champion of women's rights. Sanford served as professor of history at Swarthmore College and

An early image of the railroad station. *Image courtesy of Old Saybrook Historical Society.*

Upper Cemetery, also known as the Municipal Cemetery, is the final resting place for veterans of America's early wars. *Image courtesy of Old Saybrook Historical Society.*

taught rhetoric and elocution, literature and art history at the University of Minnesota, and she currently represents Minnesota in the U.S. Capitol's National Statuary Hall. Threatened with demolition in 2016, the home was extensively renovated and made a part of the Connecticut Cancer Foundation.

NORTH MAIN STREET AND 571 BOSTON POST ROAD

Monkey Farm

A map from 1853 shows this building as the home of H. Kirtland; it has probably been used as an inn since 1859. It was purchased in 1864 by James Coulter, and in 1892, William Coulter began serving meals from the inn and named it the Coulter House. There were a dozen rooms on the second and third floors, and it was a favorite stop for transients and traveling men. It remained in the Coulter family until 1932, when the inn's new owner, Frank Steele, changed its name to the Old Saybrook Inn. It was purchased in 1968 by Tom Davis and Harry Corning, who tended the bar there. When a previous innkeeper threw the keys to a customer and said, "Watch the place 'til I get back. I'm going to the bank," he didn't mention that the bank was in Nevada. A regular customer shouted, "They'll let anyone work here. This place is nothing but a Monkey Farm!"

1 MAIN STREET

Chamber of Commerce

This was the location of Malcolm Smith's Mobil gas station and Chrysler-Plymouth dealership. This chamber of commerce building's design is based on that of a tourist information building that was constructed in 1935, when the town commissioned architect Francis A. Nelson to design a building in honor of the town's 300th anniversary. The town provided $350 to construct the small building, which was located on the Main Street green. During World War II, the building was moved to Saybrook Point and used as a lookout spot, where locals could watch for airplanes and German submarines. The building was later used as an ice cream stand near Dock and Dine, a once-popular restaurant at Saybrook Point. The building's design was replicated on a larger scale by volunteers who constructed the current chamber of commerce building.

Above: For many years, the Coulter House was a popular stop for travelers to spend the night. Since the 1960s, it has been a restaurant known as the Monkey Farm. *Image courtesy of Old Saybrook Historical Society.*

Left: This six-foot-tall bronze statue at the head of Main Street is titled *A Boy Fishing*. It was created by artist Louise Wiley and dedicated in December 2011. *Photograph courtesy of the Old Saybrook Chamber of Commerce.*

MEDIAN DIVIDE

After a campaign in 1995 by the Garden Club to "Light Up Old Saybrook," the existing median strip on Main Street was removed, and a new brick meridian, with granite curbs and gas streetlights, was installed. The median was installed with volunteer labor and equipment; one crew began at the south end, and the other started at the north end, and in less than one long day, they met in the middle. The divider features several breaks along the way, twenty-three authentic gas lamps and accompanying planters. The plan for the median was developed by Diane Grella, and the project was supervised by contractor Robert Antoniac and Ronald Baldi from the town's department of public works.

2 MAIN STREET

Ambrose Whittlesey House

Built in 1799 by Captain Ambrose Whittlesey, a sea captain, this home is typical of many Georgian houses from the eighteenth century. Grace Pratt, the last surviving member of the Ambrose Whittlesey family to live there, obtained the house in 1919 and remained there until it was purchased in 1959 by Margaret and Linsley Shepard. "Shep" was an active local historian who, among other things, made wooden identification plaques for houses that were built before 1850. After Shep died, Margaret sold the house in 1977, and it was developed into a home furnishing store called the Marlboro Country Barn. The store expanded as the new owners obtained neighboring property. In the early 1900s, the area was the location of Watson's Drug Store, which later became a Western Union office, then a hairdressing salon, an optical store and the Endrich Insurance Agency. After long and friendly negotiations, Earl Endrich sold his property, and the building was demolished to make way for an expanded shopping complex. Known for a long time as the Saybrook Country Barn, it has become a significant gateway and important shopping complex for the town that is now known as Saybrook Home.

Proposed, promoted and, now, maintained by the Garden Club, median dividers were installed in 1995. *Photograph courtesy of Sally Perrenten.*

The Ambrose Whittlesey House became a home furnishings store in 1977. It has since grown into a shopping complex called Saybrook Home. *Image courtesy of Old Saybrook Historical Society.*

36 MAIN STREET

U.S. Post Office

As Old Saybrook and the postal service grew, the town's post office changed location several times. From the late 1930s to the postwar period, the post office was located alongside the town's movie theater. The growth of the community after World War II meant that a larger facility was needed, so a new brick building was constructed and opened in 1957 at 51 Main Street. A momentous change for the local postal service came when R.R. Donnelley, the publisher of more than one million weekly *Life* and *Time* magazines, came to town. A new post office facility was constructed across the street, at 36 Main Street, and opened in 1972.

48 MAIN STREET

Hefflon or Bannister House

This small Cape Cod–style home with large additions is known as the Hefflon House or the Bannister House. James Hefflon, a native of Newport, Rhode Island, was a farmer and butcher who moved to Saybrook and married Mary Shepherd. The couple had two boys and two girls. The house was built around 1800 by James Hefflon Sr., who died in 1842. James Jr. was a joiner, and the house remained in the family until it was sold to William Bannister in 1923.

50 MAIN STREET

Burns and Young

Robert D. Burns and Frank S. Young formed a partnership in 1890, when they purchased the business of H. Potter and Son at Saybrook Point. In 1905, they constructed the building at 50 Main Street and opened as the Burns and Young Grocery Store, which sold staple goods, canned goods, flour, paints, hardware and other items. It was a major stop for the New London–New Haven Trolley. The success of Burns and Young encouraged further commercial development along Main Street. Today, the Burns and Young building is occupied by Anytime Fitness.

This is the third Main Street location for the post office. *Photograph courtesy of Bob Czepiel.*

A general store originally located in the North Cove section of town, Burns and Young moved to Main Street in the early 1900s. *Image courtesy of Old Saybrook Historical Society.*

56 Main Street

Ingham House

This octagonal building, now known as the Ingham House, is a prefab building that is said to have been purchased from the *Sears and Roebuck Catalog* around 1890. This attribution to Sears and Roebuck is open to debate, because a number of sources indicate that the company only began offering kit houses in 1908, and apparently, such homes only became available in the United States around 1906.

The house was constructed by Horace Archer, and it was the residence of Robert Burns. Robert Burns was a partner in the nearby Burns and Young store on Main Street. His daughter, Mary Burns, lived in the house and was a postmistress for many years. While the origins of the house remain undetermined, the building, which is not a completely symmetrical octagon, has been extensively remodeled and is used as a dentist's office today.

59 Main Street

Paint Shop

This building and its business owners have been closely connected to painting and decorating since it was built in 1957 by Charles "Curly" Haynes, a painting contractor. Haynes sold the building ten years later to Gene Girdwood, who was active in the painting and decorating business. Andy Scott, the building's current owner, got his start in the painting business when he was attending the local high school. After college, he returned and purchased the business from Gene Girdwood, who was retiring. In addition to painting and decorating supplies, the store carries art supplies. The second floor of the building has been used as a meeting room for local civic organizations.

This octagonal building has been extensively altered. It is reportedly a prefabricated building from Sears Roebuck. *Image courtesy of Old Saybrook Historical Society.*

65 MAIN STREET

Elihu Ingham House

Built around 1795, this is one of the few original eighteenth-century buildings that remains in the commercial section of Main Street. Its gambrel roof and classic porticos that flank the front door are evidence of the building's early origin. The Ward family moved into the home in 1932, and Pauline Ward later became active in the affairs of the Republican Party. A candy business was started by Ed Ward's father, and they made and sold candy under the name of Ye Old Saybrooke Sweets and Old Saybrook Candies. Later, the candy was made elsewhere, but it was still sold at this location. The candy was initially packaged in mahogany boxes, which were later replaced by inexpensive paper and cardboard. Since the 1960s, the building has been used as the real estate office of Schlag and Snow, the Vander Brooke Bakery and other commercial operations.

118 MAIN STREET

Fiorelli's Home Furnishings

This was the site of a popular bowling alley; many area leagues played there before it was closed around 1950 and became the site of Fiorelli's Home Furnishings, which remained open until 1984. Lou Fiorelli began working at Pratt-Read & Co. in Deep River, which produced wooden gliders during World War II for the army and navy. In 1943, he entered active military service as a carpenter in the U.S. Army Air Corps. After the war, Lou and his father began designing and crafting high-quality furniture, and they opened their Main Street store, which sold upholstered furniture and living and dining room sets. After the store was closed, the building remained vacant for a while before it was divided; today, it houses Essex Golf and Seaside Liquor.

132 MAIN STREET

Saybrook Hardware (Dudley Block)

Ever since A.L. "Dud" Dudley completed this building in 1929, it has been known as the Dudley Block and has always included a hardware store. When it was constructed, across the street from the Dudley Dodge-Plymouth Garage and Lodging House, the Dudley Block was a significant addition to Main Street commerce. Among its first occupants was Watson's Drugstore, which had relocated from the head of Main Street, the A&P building. Dudley then took the store next to the A&P and made it into an automobile showroom; adjoining this was the town's new hardware and electrical goods store that was opened by Charles King. Later, the Dudley Block was the location of Dan Adanti's Bar and Grill, Saybrook Liquor, the town's first radio and TV store, a five-and-ten-cent store, a dress shop, a flower shop and the chamber of commerce.

Today, the hardware store occupies almost the entire building. The store was first run by the King family, and in 1965, Ann Sawyer sold the business to George and Barbara Maynard. George was a farmer, carpenter and builder, and Barbara was first selectwoman. The couple doubled the size of the store, and it was soon considered to have one of the largest and most

This building was opened as Fiorelli's Home Furnishings, which featured upholstered furniture, as well as living and dining room sets, until owner Lou Fiorelli retired in 1984. In recent years, it has been divided into a liquor store and sport clothing store. *Image courtesy of Old Saybrook Historical Society.*

Built in 1928, the Dudley Building has been the location of the hardware store ever since. For many years, "Ozzie" (2004–2018) provided an unofficial welcome. *Photograph courtesy of Sally Perrenten.*

varied inventories in the area. The store's employees, then and now, have been well known for helping solve homeowner problems. The Maynards ran the business for twenty years before they retired and sold the store to Patrick and Virginia Plant from Florida and Essex in 1985. Some residents think that the hardware store may be the oldest continuing business in town. The most recent owners are Brian and Kate Toolan.

154 MAIN STREET

Malloy's

This one-floor commercial building was built in 1941. For many years, it was known as Malloy's Five and Dime Store and offered a wide variety of inexpensive products. It was opened by Ed Malloy in 1960, and it was bought by William Moshier two years later; they worked together until Ed retired in 1986. The store was closed for good in 1990. "This type of business moved off into the sunset," observed Bill Moshier. Part of Malloy's charm was its out-of-date merchandise that had the ability to transport customers back to their youths. The building was occupied by CVS Pharmacy until 2017, when the vacant storefront was filled by physicians from Middlesex Hospital.

161 MAIN STREET

St. John R.C. Church and Rectory

The parish began as a mission of St. Joseph's Church in Chester in 1884, and it became a separate parish in 1914. Its original location was just north of the railroad station, where the cemetery remains today. A piece of land was obtained by the Saybrook parish on Main Street, and a new church constructed there in the early 1930s. At the corner of Main and Maynard Streets was the Gift Mart and Scots Shop, a gift and yarn shop that was housed in the converted home of Elisha Hart, but in the 1960s, the home was demolished and replaced by St. John's parish house.

166 MAIN STREET

Saybrook Theater

From 1728 to 1928, this was the site of the Azariah Mather House. Mather was the fourth minister of Old Saybrook's Congregational church and was a direct descendant of Cotton and Increase Mather from the Massachusetts Bay Colony. A six-hundred-seat motion picture theater was built on the site in 1937 by Leo Bonoff of Madison, and the following year, when the U.S. Postal Service was looking for a new and larger facility, Bonoff won the bid, causing considerable local antagonism, and built additions on both sides of the theater. The new post office was located here, along with Young's Soda Shop and Fred's Beauty Shop. The building was renovated in 2005, and it became the site of professional offices and Liv's Oyster Bar.

Top: St. John R.C. Church in Old Saybrook was founded in 1884. A parochial school was established in 1994. *Image courtesy of Old Saybrook Historical Society.*

Bottom: Built in 1937, with pillars and a dome, the theater closed in 2002 and was converted into retail space. *Image courtesy of Old Saybrook Historical Society.*

178 Main Street

Walt's Market

This popular meat market was long known as the place where Katharine Hepburn, often let in by the back door, navigated the narrow aisles, pushing the store's notoriously undersized carts. Her privacy was protected by all of Main Street's shopkeepers. The market had been owned and operated by Walt Kozey since the late 1950s, when he became the owner of the Universal Food Store. The market was known for its fresh products and good prices, with the aromas and atmosphere of an old-fashioned meat market. Second- and third-generation customers have been greeted by Walt's son Paul since the mid-1990s.

186 Main Street

Hallisey's Pharmacy

Robert Hallisey opened his pharmacy in 1963 and continued operating it for forty years before retiring and going to work at the CVS Pharmacy. Bob Hallisey was admired as a personal and friendly pharmacist, and he was deeply involved in many civic affairs. He was president of the Main Street Business Association when the Saybrook Stroll was started. He was also the president of the High School Music Boosters and a member of the board of education, the planning commission, the nursing board and the Westbrook Elks.

196 Main Street

Porter Plaza

This five-and-a-half-acre, four-building, fourteen-store shopping area was developed by New Haven real estate entrepreneur Henry Porter in 1981. Often referred to today as Porter Plaza, the site is more properly known as Willbrook, named after brothers William and Brooks Childress. Much of the

For well over fifty years, Walt's has been a popular local landmark that is known for its old-fashioned atmosphere and butcher shop. Next door was Hallisey's Pharmacy, which was opened in 1963 and remained in business for forty years. Robert Hallisey was the president of the Main Street Business Association, which started the Saybrook Stroll. *Image courtesy of Old Saybrook Historical Society.*

The Great Atlantic & Pacific Tea Company, better known as A&P, was started in 1859, but by the end of the 1900s, it was unable to compete. This site was purchased and repurposed to hold a movie theater and several retail shops. *Image courtesy of Old Saybrook Historical Society.*

shopping complex is located on the former site of an A&P Store, which had been vacant for more than a year. The site's original plans called for small, upscale shopping boutiques, and its early stores included Hair Unlimited, Poor Richards and Season's Desires. These stores were followed by Western Auto, Hallmark Cards, Kid Stuff and Lace and Lingerie. At one time, it was the location for a movie theater, and today, it is the location of the Estuary Center, a provider of services for mature area residents.

201 MAIN STREET

Jas. Jay Smith Real Estate

This building was the home of the real estate office of Jas. Jay Smith and, later, his son Avy B. Smith. The Jas. Jay Smith Company had summer offices in more than a half-dozen shoreline towns and developed several beach communities along the shoreline. Its headquarters were in New York City and on Main Street in Old Saybrook. In 1979, the building became the home and office of Attorney Michael E. Cronin Jr.

211 MAIN STREET

Frontier Communications

The first telephone exchange in Old Saybrook was opened in 1895, with Clara Kimball as the manager and her living room as the location of the switchboard. In 1925, increased demand caused the operation to be moved to a new building with a ten-position switchboard just north of the railroad tracks. The switchboards and their female operators were then moved to a new building on Main Street in 1940. The colonial-style brick building housed the Southern New England Telephone Company's business departments, as well as its switching systems and operator services, until 1973, when many of the services were moved into a new office at 36 Lynde Street (now the police department building). G. Fred King, the first selectman from 1946 to 1955, was the manager of the business office. The Main Street building now houses the operations of Frontier Communications.

Jas. Jay Smith had offices on Main Street and was one of largest developers of summer homes along the shoreline. *Image courtesy of Old Saybrook Historical Society.*

Originally the Southern New England Telephone Company, this building was transferred to Frontier Communications in 2013. *Image courtesy of Old Saybrook Historical Society.*

226 MAIN STREET

Dr. Aaron M. Greenberg

This large, stately home served as the residence of Aaron (1906–82) and Adeline Greenberg, and it served as Aaron's family physician's office from 1932 to 1983. A graduate of New York University and the Long Island School of Medicine, Aaron was also the school physician and medical examiner for the town of Old Saybrook. He was a leader in organizing the chamber of commerce and a first chairman of the Parks and Recreation Commission and was instrumental in getting the town's first ambulance. The house was built about 1888 by Gad Baldwin. The building and surrounding property have since been developed by Jerry Brophy into more than a dozen condominiums that were designed to preserve the property's historic features.

266 MAIN STREET

Rochette Building

W.W. Rochette, a Saybrook contractor, and Frank Palmer of Hartford purchased the land on the corner of Sheffield Street and in 1930 built a group of stores, including Joseph Ranelli's Rexall Drug Store, where generations of students enjoyed the soda fountain, with milkshakes and black and white sodas. Later, many had their first jobs here. Ranelli's later moved to a larger space next door and was renamed Central Pharmacy. Many townspeople stopped into Central Pharmacy to pick up their newspaper and exchange town news. The building also included a supermarket, a print shop operated by Reverend Elkins and his family and a restaurant.

274 AND 276 MAIN STREET

Stokes Bros. Building

This brick building, which was perhaps built in the mid-1800s as the Sheffield and Sons store, was later owned by T.C. Acton Jr. and is more popularly

Left: Home and office of Dr. Aaron Greenberg. Today, the building and surrounding area have been converted to condominiums. *Image courtesy of Old Saybrook Historical Society.*

Below: This one-story building has been the home of multiple businesses, including a bakery, a baby clothing store, a dance center, a painting company, a printing shop, a sausage shop and a tavern. *Image courtesy of Old Saybrook Historical Society.*

known as the location of the Stokes Brothers General Store. Herb and Fred Stokes clerked for their uncle Giles Bushnell and later bought his dry goods business. For a time, Herb joined forces with George Kirtland under the name of Stokes and Kirtland, but it became Stokes Brothers General Store when Fred rejoined his brother. Dr. Wolfe served the entire community as a dentist from his office on the second floor. The Stokes brothers ran their business for thirty-three years before retiring in 1945, when they sold the business to Alfred and Dominic Tiezzi. The Tiezzis also owned and operated the Silver Street Restaurant, as well as the Evergreen Inn, both of which were on Main Street. The Stokes brothers were noted for their generosity, integrity and the homespun quality of friendliness, which made the store a popular gathering place. In recent years, the building has been the location of a barbershop and a liquor store, and it has apartments on the second floor.

286 Main Street

Gilt Edge Restaurant

It is believed that this building dates back to pre-Revolutionary years, due to the beautiful chestnut-pegged beams. Originally, it was a school with a blacksmith shop in the rear. During the early 1900s, it was known as the Gilt Edge and included a pool room, a hamburger and soda shop and a set of hand-cranked gasoline pumps in front of the restaurant—the local embodiment of a genuine greasy spoon. It was owned and operated by justice of the peace Tom Kerwin. It was the only place between New Haven and New London that was open for twenty-four hours daily, and it attracted, not surprisingly, many long-haul truck drivers. Since the 1960s, it has been the location of various restaurants, including, most recently, the Red Hen.

287 Main Street

Humphrey Pratt Tavern

This structure, built around 1785, was owned by the same family until 1943, when it was sold to boat builder J.W. Stueck. It was a stage stop on the route

This was one of the town's earliest brick buildings, and it was used as a store in 1853. Known then as the Sheffield Building, it became the location of Stokes General Store. *Photograph courtesy of Sally Perrenten.*

The Humphrey Pratt Tavern, now a private residence, was the site of the town's first post office and a visit from the Marquis de Lafayette in 1824. *Photograph courtesy of Robert Czepiel.*

between New Haven and Boston, and it served as Saybrook's first post office. Ordination balls were held in this building after the installation of each new minister. Its notable architectural features include its second-floor ballroom, which has a spring floor to facilitate dancing. The Marquis de Lafayette stayed overnight at the tavern during his triumphant tour of the United States in 1824. He reportedly made a purchase in the adjacent general store, which was built in 1790 and, later, moved down the street and renamed James Pharmacy and Soda Fountain. Humphrey Pratt was a brother of deacon Timothy Pratt, whose house stands nearby.

288 MAIN

Patrick's Country Store

Merle Patrick opened his country store, sometimes known as "the little town hall," in the early 1930s, when he took over the Economy Market. It became a community gathering place and drew customers and friends of all ages. Patrick started by selling dry goods and eventually expanded his inventory to include practically everything—clothing, school supplies, newspapers, boots, pots and pans, overalls, crabbing nets and a free bag of candy (spearmint leaves, chocolate babies, jawbreakers, root beer barrels, et cetera) for students with good report cards. The ownership of the store was passed to Betty and Bob Van Zant, and in 1985, it was passed to Barry Maynard. A fixture in town for many years, the store was closed in the mid-1980s, a victim of changing shopping patterns, malls, discount and factory stores and catalogs.

292 MAIN STREET

Esty's

This is perhaps the oldest commercial store on Main Street. It was first established by W.H. Smith as his Stove and Tin Ware Store in 1874. A second floor with an exterior staircase was added in 1912 and is still present today; it became an apartment that was most notably occupied by Kathleen Goodwin, the elementary school principal for whom the school

William Smith opened Smith's Stove and Tin Ware, today's Esty's, one of the town's oldest continuously owned buildings operated as a store. Nearby stores included the Economy Market, the Gilt Edge restaurant and Stokes Brothers Groceries, Hardware and Paint Store. *Image courtesy of Old Saybrook Historical Society.*

was named. Smith was active in local politics and was a first selectman. His son Gordon succeeded him in both owning the store and also becoming a first selectman, as did his son Malcolm in 1965. The building housed Fred Beebe's Electric Store in the 1950s and was later opened as an electrical and lamp store by Irving Esty. The store has since been run by his family and, today, offers a variety of ornamental household products and sells and repairs lamps.

300 MAIN STREET

Katharine Hepburn Cultural Arts Center

Named after the famous actress and local resident, the Katharine Hepburn Cultural Arts Center, or the Kate, was opened in 2009. It was originally constructed in 1910 and 1911 and served as the town hall. It later served as

Presentation of the flag at the town hall, circa 1921. *Image courtesy of Old Saybrook Historical Society.*

a theater after a successful effort was led by Joseph Cone, a printer, author and musical performer, to form the Musical and Dramatic Club and raise funds to construct a theater for performances. It has served as the home for the Musical and Dramatic Club's theatrical performances and lectures, as a basketball court while the school next door was being built and as the town hall, which included a jail on the lower level. After the town hall was moved to the former elementary school next door in 2004, residents voted to restore the original building and open it as a cultural arts center named after the actress.

302 MAIN STREET

Town Hall

Old Saybrook's Main Street School was built with Works Progress Administration (WPA) funds in 1936, replacing the wooden 1892 Consolidated

School. The school's eight classrooms and large auditorium were designed to serve students from kindergarten through the twelfth grade. As the town's population grew, a new junior high school was built, followed by an elementary school. This building served as the town's high school until a new one was built on the Boston Post Road in the 1960s. In 1999, voters approved a referendum to convert the building into a new town hall, while also restoring the old town hall and turning it into the Katharine Hepburn Cultural Arts Center.

To honor World War I veterans, a granite memorial was erected on town property near the Coulter House in 1926, and it was moved to the town green when Route 1 was realigned. Today, memorials to the veterans of World War II and the Vietnam War are also located on the green. For a time, the green sported a cannon and a tourist information building. A bandstand was designed by architect Robert Wendler and constructed by the Lions Club. The high school band, under the direction of John Torrenti, performed in its dedication ceremony in 1978.

Both the town hall and school were very much a part of Main Street life. *Image courtesy of Old Saybrook Historical Society.*

310 MAIN STREET

Fire Department

Organized in 1924, the fire department's first and only fire engine was a donated American LaFrance chemical engine, and it was housed in a shed behind the town hall. The town's first fire chief was Gordon Smith. A larger shed was built in the 1930s, but it was razed in the 1990s to provide more space for parking. A larger, two-story station was constructed in the late 1930s, and the present firehouse was built in 1961. While the town owns the firehouse and equipment, the company is a volunteer organization.

MAIN AND OLD BOSTON POST ROAD

Public Well

The public well, which was re-created in recent years, was provided by the Saybrook Town Improvement Association "for the accommodation of man and beast." Horses drank from the trough, and people drew well water with a rotary hand crank that had small cups attached to an endless chain. Directly behind the pump was the home of Captain Morgan, which became Ye Old Say-Brooke Inn. In 1964, the home was demolished to make way for Ed's Enterprises and, now, various commercial enterprises.

325 MAIN STREET AND PENNYWISE LANE

James Pharmacy and Deacon Timothy Pratt House

In the late 1700s and early 1800s, the pharmacy was part of the Humphrey Pratt Tavern and served as a general store until it was moved to its present location. The building is best known as the home of the pharmacy that was owned by Miss Anna L. James, the first African American woman pharmacist in Connecticut. Rumor has it that General Lafayette made a purchase at the store when it was part of the Humphrey Pratt House at the corner of Old Boston Post Road and Main Street.

The fire station, first used in the 1920s, was located behind the town hall. *Photograph courtesy Old Saybrook Fire Department.*

The old town pump included metal cups attached to a revolving chain and a horse trough. *Image courtesy of Old Saybrook Historical Society.*

From this building, Anna Louise James, who was always known locally as Miss James, lived and ran her pharmacy. Next door was the Deacon Timothy Pratt Tavern, which has served as a bed-and-breakfast in recent years. *Image courtesy of Old Saybrook Historical Society.*

Timothy Pratt was a carpenter and a deacon in the Congregational church, and he built this house around 1746. At one time, the house may have been used as a school. It was purchased in 1856 by James Treadway, who used it as a residence known as the Treadway Place. After Treadway's death, his widow, Lucy, rented the store to Peter Lane in 1895; he later opened an apothecary shop there.

When Lucy died in 1899, Virginia Freeman inherited both buildings and continued to rent to Lane. In 1913, Anna L. James partnered with her brother-in-law Peter Lane, took over the pharmacy and lived upstairs. In 1922, a two-story wing was added to the pharmacy, and Miss James purchased the Treadway Home and the pharmacy. She sold the Treadway Home to Helen Roberts in 1927. Miss James was hardworking and highly respected. She retired in 1967 and died in 1977, at the age of ninety-one. The James estate sold the building in 1979, and it has changed hands several times. The building retained its famous ice cream parlor until recent years, when it has mostly been used as an eating establishment.

334 Main Street

Samuel H. Pratt House

Though this home is not as ornate as other houses from the Victorian era, it does have some of the ornamental details that are associated with nineteenth-century architecture, including decorative eaves, a porch and large windows. Today, the building is used for housing by Grace Church.

336 Main Street

Grace Episcopal Church and Rectory

The current church building was constructed with locally mined granite in 1872, and it is best described as an English Gothic–style building. Its arches and buttresses provide the look of a small medieval cathedral. Regular Episcopal services began to be held in Old Saybrook in 1825, and the first church was constructed in 1830 and 1831. It was later replaced by the current church, which was constructed in 1871 and 1872. The old church house, located on the Old Boston Post Road, became a post office and J.A. Ayer's Boot and Shoe Store, and it is still used today. The first rectory was built around 1873 and was a copy of a house that Reverend Jesse Heald saw in England. It was lost to a fire, and the replacement, which is still used today, was constructed in 1892.

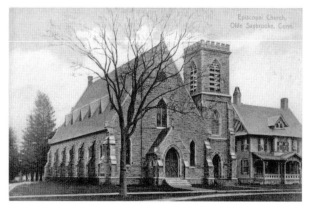

This English Gothic–style building, constructed in 1872, was designed by Reverend Jesse Heald, and its stone came from the town quarry located near today's Staples office supply store on the Boston Post Road. *Image courtesy of Old Saybrook Historical Society.*

341 MAIN STREET

P.L. Shephard House

Built around 1810 by Nathaniel Clarke, this house was remodeled and moved to its current location around 1850. The low ceiling and hall arrangement inside the house, as well as the geometric arrangement of its front windows, are indicators of Colonial architecture. The mansard roof and ornate eyebrow dormers indicate that there were later alterations, probably around the time that the structure served as the Seabury Institute (1875), a private military school for young boys. The building to the rear of the house, which has somewhat compatible architecture, was part of the school's facilities.

350 MAIN STREET

General William Hart House

William Hart Jr. built this home for his bride, Esther Buckingham, in 1767. Hart was a merchant engaged in trade in the West Indies. During the Revolutionary War, he outfitted privateers and led the First Regiment of Connecticut Light Horse Militia to Danbury when that town was raided by the British. After the war, he successfully speculated in land in the Western Reserve and was a candidate for governor of Connecticut multiple times. The house has typical twelve-over-twelve windows, a center hallway and twin chimneys; its corner chimneys, however, are unique. The interior has wide floorboards, old wainscoting and paneling. The house was later purchased by the Old Saybrook Historical Society and restored to its original authenticity. The home has since been used as the society's headquarters, a museum, exhibit gallery and meeting place for various public programs.

366 MAIN STREET

First Church of Christ, Congregational

This building was constructed in 1840, and it was extensively renovated in 1977. It is the fourth church building of the congregation; the first two

A minister at the Grace Episcopal Church and a former instructor at the school conducted by Hetty Hart, Reverend Peter Shepard opened this boarding and military school in 1867. *Photograph courtesy of Robert Czepiel.*

Built in 1767 by William Hart, this building is listed in the National Register of Historic Places. Hart later became a notable merchant, a veteran of the American Revolution, a speculator in western lands and a candidate for governor. *Photograph courtesy of Robert Lorenz.*

Congregational Church, Saybrook, Conn.

Originally founded at Saybrook Fort in 1646, this Congregational church was constructed in 1840. The parish house next door was relocated and is now a private residence. *Image courtesy of Old Saybrook Historical Society.*

are located at Saybrook Point, and the third meeting house was built in 1726, across from what is known as the Church Green or Trivet Green. The sides were reportedly built flat on the ground and lifted by a team of twenty oxen before they were placed in deep troughs to lift the entire side. This was one of the first prefab churches in the country.

The congregation benefitted from several notable and long-serving ministers, including Thomas Buckingham (1665–1709), William Hart (1736–83) and Frederick William Hotchkiss (1783–1844). Thomas Buckingham played a leading role in the founding of the Collegiate School in 1701 that later became Yale College. In 1708, Buckingham was also a leader of a group of ministers that formulated the Saybrook Platform, a doctrine that established the standards for Congregational church governance.

Next to the church was the parsonage, which was built in 1875 and served as a parish house. It was moved in 1990 by James Magoon, a contractor, and renovated into a residence.

381 Main Street

Fred Beebe House and Studio 381

This house, built around 1874, was the residence of Fred and Alice Beebe, and it is also sometimes referred to as the Justin B. Holman House, as Holman was an earlier owner. Fred Beebe was noted for his hobby of making and showing hometown movies, and he could be found throughout the year at most public events with his camera. He and Alice enjoyed showing the films in their basement, which they called Cinema 381. There, they showed films of local events, cartoons and assorted old-time favorites. They created a thirty-five-by-twelve-foot theater, with a ten-foot-high ceiling, by dredging and waterproofing their basement. They removed the cellar hatchway and built an enclosure for the main entrance and marquee. The stage was six feet high and eight feet long. For seating, the couple used old theater seats from the town hall. Intermissions at the theater were filled with popcorn, and guests could browse the couple's personal collection of autographed pictures of favorite movie stars.

395 Main Street

Samuel Hart House

Built around 1773 by Samuel Hart, a son of Reverend William Hart and brother of General William Hart, the home's center chimney construction is typical of the Colonial era. The house was purchased in 1971 by the Old Saybrook Historical Society, and several exhibits were installed. Some three years later, the Historical Society sold the Samuel Hart House and purchased the General William Hart House from the Congregational church.

404 Main Street

John Shipman House

This house is shown on early maps and has been dated to 1687 or 1697. By the mid-1700s, it was owned by John Shipman. It has been altered over the years, but it retains four original fireplaces and a beehive oven in the kitchen.

412 MAIN STREET

Joseph Buckingham House

The owners believe it was built in the late seventeenth century, and that theory is supported by the home's architectural style. It has the general proportions of a lean-to saltbox, but the windows are typical of an eighteenth-century Colonial house. Long known as the Old Buckingham House or the Joseph Buckingham House, the home was likely built as early as 1671. It was once the home of Reverend Thomas Buckingham, one of Yale's original founders and trustees. It is believed to have been moved to its current location and was perhaps the site of the first Yale commencement in 1702.

500 MAIN STREET

Samuel Eliot House

This home was built around 1737 by either Dr. Samuel Eliot or, perhaps, his brother Dr. Augustus Eliot. They were the sons of Jared Eliot, who died in 1747. The home was purchased by Captain Samuel Lord in 1749. Lord then sold the home to his son-in-law, Captain Jabez Stow Sr., who served in the American Revolution and died in 1785. Stow's son, Jabez Stow Jr., was lost at sea in 1788, and the house was then occupied by Stow Jr.'s daughter Mary Stow, who married Captain David Newell in 1784. Captain Newell was engaged in the slave trade and was reportedly killed during an uprising of the slaves on board his vessel in the Cape Verde Islands in 1819. The house became the residence of Yale University professor Edward P. Morris, who restored it in 1928.

BEYOND MAIN STREET

Main Street runs in a straight line toward Long Island Sound, although the name changes to College Street. It is the path to several sites of historic importance. After passing the early mill stone, which is enclosed by an iron fence, a traveler quickly reaches a modest fork in the road, and as Yogi Berra famously suggested, they should take it. To the left is North Cove Road, a quiet half loop that returns to the main road; it is the location of several early seafarer's homes and old wharf sites.

The main road, at this point College Street, includes the Yale Boulder, which marked the beginning of Yale College in 1701, when it was known as the Collegiate School. Next to the Yale Boulder is Cypress Cemetery, which is listed in the National Register of Historic Places and is the burial site of Lady Fenwick and many local dignitaries.

Just beyond the cemetery is Saybrook Fort Monument Park. Here, a small marker commemorates the arrival of George Fenwick. An impressive statue of Lion Gardiner, the military engineer who built Saybrook Fort and laid out a town for the expected arrival of English noblemen who never came, is also located in the park. The park includes an outline of the fort, although the actual location was closer to the high point in the North Cove area. A bit farther south is the early twentieth-century site of the roundhouse for the Valley Shore Railroad.

In the far corner of the parking area is Gardiner's Landing, a pleasant park area overlooking the Connecticut River and Long Island Sound. Throughout the area are markers providing historic and environmental information. At the water's edge is the town's pavilion, a public facility used for meetings and social events. Here, too, is Saybrook Resort and Marina, a site that has a long and colorful history and, now, the town's premier resort and restaurant. In symbolism and reality, this short, straight road holds the history of the people who lived here. It's the story of one Main Street. It's the story of all Main Streets.

2

"NARROWVILLE" WITH THE WAYBACKERS

*I*n a warm-hearted book about characters in a town called Narrowville, author Joe Cone (1869–1918) wrote, "There was no manufacturing in Narrowville, unless we make exception of the fairly prosperous 'yarn' industry, which was carried on at the leading village store. Here, yarns were spun unceasingly." His book *The Waybackers* reflects on the lives and times of many small towns in 1905, the year in which he wrote the book. Cone provides sketches of common folks that are humorous, clever, perceptive and reflect human nature. Even today, his descriptions of everyday life contain flashes of insight that are inescapably familiar.

Joe Cone was born in East Haddam, Connecticut, and was a direct descendant of Daniel Cone, one of the town's first settlers. By the time he was fifteen years old, Cone went to work making fish nets for the American Net and Twine Company. In his spare time, he played cornet in the Moodus and East Haddam cornet bands. Four years after he began working, the American Net and Twine Company moved to East Cambridge, Massachusetts, and took nineteen-year-old Joe with it. There, he became the head machinist and draftsman. Two years later, he married his childhood sweetheart, Emma Elizabeth Clevenshire. Joe was good at his job, so the company sent him to work in Chicago and, later, Baltimore. By the time he was twenty-eight years old, he had learned mechanical drawing and was the foreman responsible for building special machinery; in the meantime, he was also taking an English course at Harvard.

Aerial view of Main Street from the south. *Photograph courtesy of Robert Czepiel.*

Joe was attracted to poetry, writing, drawing and music, and from time to time, he wrote for Boston and Connecticut newspapers and various magazines. Even before moving to Saybrook, Joe had gained some recognition for his cheerful writings, and his poems were even published in Boston newspapers and national magazines, including *Life*, *Judge* and *Puck*. In 1899, Joe started a magazine called *Little Joker and Storyist*, and in the same year, he published a book of poems called *Heart and Home Ballads*. For several years, he wrote a daily column of poems and commentary for the *Boston Herald* called "Uncle Ezra Sez." During this productive time, Joe contributed to newspapers like the *New York Sun* and magazines, including the *Pictorial Review*, *Youth's Companion*, *Suburban Life*, *Christian Endeavor World* and *Connecticut Magazine*. Joe's active mind and creative talent ultimately caused him to leave the American Net and Twine Company in 1904. He then moved to Old Saybrook, where he purchased a home at 108 Old Boston Post Road; the house had a small outbuilding, which he used as an office for writing. The outbuilding was also where he started the Old Saybrook Print Shop. He found fertile ground in Saybrook for his energy and writing.

After a meeting in his home in 1905, he, along with many members of the Old Saybrook Cornet Band, including baritone horn players and proprietors of the town's largest grocery store Herbert and Frederick Stokes, and alto horn player and director of the Deep River National Bank Giles Bushnell, organized the Musical and Dramatic Club "to raise a fund for the purpose of purchasing land and building a public hall thereon." The club was incorporated in November 1906 and began raising money by presenting plays, operettas, concerts and suppers. Joe, his wife, Emma, and their daughter, Irene,

Joseph Cone (1869–1918) was a leader in forming the Old Saybrook Musical and Dramatic Club, which raised funds to purchase land and build the town hall. *Image courtesy of Old Saybrook Historical Society.*

Joe Cone returning from the Post Office with a pocketful of de-jected manuscripts.

This image is of a character from Joe Cone's book *The Waybackers*. *Image courtesy of Old Saybrook Historical Society.*

performed in some of the plays. Among the club's large donors was Morgan Gardner Bulkeley, who was born and raised in East Haddam and had a summer home in Fenwick. Finally, on May 26, 1911, a Colonial Revival–style brick building was completed and dedicated at a cost of $20,000. That building is today's Katharine Hepburn Cultural Arts Center.

One notable instance of Joe's earthy humor occurred at a time when automobile manufacturing was a competitive and serious industry in Connecticut. After the prominent Pope Company closed in Hartford, many other companies also decided to end production. Many of these firms were threatened with legal action from Henry Ford for trumped-up charges of patent infringement. To expose these underhanded tactics, Cone placed an announcement in the newspaper stating that he had been accepted as the local agent for the Hess Mobile, a nonexistent car that was actually a wind-up toy made in Germany. It wasn't long before the announcement came to the attention of Ford, who sent a letter threatening to sue. "Our attorneys inform us that, in some important mechanical features, the Hess Mobile infringes upon patents owned and controlled by the Ford Motor Car Company, and I therefore warn you against further attempts at demonstration and sale under penalty of legal prosecution." For his part, Joe Cone then wrote "The Twentieth Century 23rd Psalm."

The Ford is my auto;
I shall not want (another).
It maketh me lie down beneath it;
It anointeth my clothes with oil;
It soreth my soul.
Yea, though I ride through the valleys,
I am towed up the hills;
I fear much evil,
For its rods and its engine discomfort me;
I anoint its tires with patches;
Its radiator runneth over,
I repair its blowouts in the presence of mine enemies.
Surely, if this thing followed me all the days of my life,
I shall dwell in the bughouse forever.

During World War I, Cone put his mechanical skills to work making submarine engines at the New London Ship and Engine Company in Groton (today, this company is the Electric Boat Company). At the same time, he wrote nearly two dozen Home Guard ballads that were published by the *New London Day*, and he was the chief bugler in the Saybrook Home Guard.

In support of the war effort, he wrote a short poem called "Pen, or Musket."

> *I've a pen and I've a musket,*
> *And I'm full of pep, I am,*
> *And in case of war I offer*
> *Either one to Uncle Sam.*
> *I can launch a round of poems*
> *That would win most any scrap.*
> *If my Uncle wants the musket,*
> *The musket it shall be;*
> *If he thinks the verse more fatal,*
> *Let him leave the verse to me.*

Shortly after, Joe suddenly took ill and was operated on for an intestinal obstruction at the Hospital St. Raphael in New Haven. The procedure was not successful, and his short life of forty-eight years came to an end on March 29, 1918. The *New London Day* reported that "fifty members of the Home Guard, of which he was the chief bugler, marched at the head of the funeral party to the First Congregational Church, which was crowded to its full capacity by friends." Reverend William F. White conducted the funeral service, which included a reading of Cone's favorite poem, "The House on the Side of the Road." Joe's friends from Stokes General Store— Captain John A. Ayer, Dr. William H. Wolfe, Herbert B. Stokes and William R. Bushnell—served as pallbearers for his burial at Riverview Cemetery.

Newton Newkirk wrote in the *Boston Post*:

> *Joe just couldn't help writing, and when he wrote, he couldn't help being cheerful and optimistic....His lines always breathed "help and hope" and courage. And that's why people read what he wrote and clipped his lines to carry around in their pocketbooks or paste in their scrapbooks.*
>
> *Au revoir, Joe, old friend—au revoir and good luck on the long journey. If there is a tear in my eye, it is a tear of gratitude for your good humor and your comradeship. You lived to the end your creed of cheerfulness, and the world is better and brighter because you tarried in it. So, bon voyage, Joe—good luck and God bless you.*

Cone's granddaughter Anne Sweet was known to many Saybrook residents as an authority on early Native American life and as the co-author of *In the Shade of Sayebrooke Fort*. She was a volunteer at the Old Saybrook Historical Society for many years and a valued resource for historic information on numerous topics.

3.

VILLAGE OF ELMS

*I*f a traveling salesman came to town, peddling a potent elixir that could cool us in summer, warm us in winter, provide food, prevent erosion, cleanse the air and offer a home for songbirds and inspire poets, I'm guessing that most reasonable people would say "bring it on." To obtain this magic tonic, you need to only plant a seed and provide it with water, sunlight and a little tender, loving care. The catch is that you have to do this for the next generation, just as the earlier generations had done for you. We are talking about trees, of course, and the earlier inhabitants of Old Saybrook knew and understood their great value and beauty. They understood the significance of the old Chinese expression, "The best time to plant a tree was twenty years ago. The next best time is now."

Of all the tree varieties, the elm has a special relationship with life in Old Saybrook. In fact, around the turn of the last century, with its tree-lined, canopy-covered Main Street, Old Saybrook was popularly called the village of elms. The town has been populated with tree lovers and huggers for some time. In the mid-1800s, at the house of Elisha Hart, which stood near the current site of the rectory for St. John's Church on Main Street, there were three majestic elms that Elisha reverently called Abraham, Isaac and Jacob. As the son of the Reverend William Hart, the pastor of the Congregational church for forty-five years, this identification was, perhaps, not surprising.

On Arbor Day 1895, students at the graded school planted ten elms and named them after the founding trustees of Yale College in Saybrook: Noyes, Chauncey, Buckingham, Andrew, Woodridge, Webb, Pierson, Mather,

A visitor in 1902 observed that "lines of great elms and sugar maples shadowed the walks, and the latter had blossomed so that every little twig had its tassels." *Image courtesy of Old Saybrook Historical Society.*

Pierpont and Russell. The trees remained until 1946, when they had to be replaced with Norway maples.

In 1906, the Town Improvement Association planted elms on Main and College Streets to Saybrook Point. But the most notable tree-caring instance of the town's farsighted ancestors occurred on the one hundredth anniversary of the signing of the Declaration of Independence, July 4, 1876. An eight-man committee was appointed, and fifty dollars was appropriated "to purchase and locate fifty-six elm trees within the highways of the town, said trees to be known and cared for by the town as 'Centennial Trees.'" The fifty-six trees represented the signers of the Declaration of Independence. An equal number of trees were planted within each of the town's four school districts: Saybrook Point, Oyster River, the Ferry District and the center.

The tall, graceful, stately elms eventually provided a storybook picture of New England village charm. However, by 1976, one hundred years after they were planted, Dutch elm disease, the 1938 hurricane, the chainsaw and "progress" had claimed all but a handful. Today, five of the original centennial elms remain. They can be seen on Main Street in the town green near the firehouse; on the Boston Post Road in front of the McDonald's restaurant; in front of a private residence on Ragged Rock Road East; at a

Another visitor stated that the "splendid highway, with smooth macadam surface, [extended] through the town to Saybrook Point." *Image courtesy of Old Saybrook Historical Society.*

private residence on the banks of North Cove; and on Main Street, in front of Saybrook Home. At Saybrook Home, a few seedlings have dropped from the elm into the Constitution Garden and sprouted. Some have been nurtured by longtime Garden Club members Judy Glover and former selectwoman Barbara J. Maynard, and they are being planted as they mature.

The town has had a tree committee since 1998. After starting with the help of selectman Bill Peace, the committee has planted hundreds of trees, but in recent years, it has been relatively inactive. 'Tis time to plant again.

4

THE LINES AT THE JUNCTION

*A*s an architectural masterpiece, the Saybrook Railroad Station doesn't quite match the beauty and grandeur of New York's Grand Central Station or Washington, D.C.'s Union Station, but since its construction, which was completed just after the last spike was driven in the Transcontinental Railroad (1869), it has adapted to change and served its modest purpose. On May 22, 1830, not long after George Stephenson built a locomotive capable of traveling at thirty miles per hour, thereby ending the commonly held belief that people would die of asphyxiation at those speeds, early railroad passenger service began at the Mount Clare station of the Baltimore and Ohio Railroad. This station was also the site of the first telegraph message by Samuel F.B. Morse, a sometime resident of Saybrook, in 1844.

In Connecticut, on July 1, 1852, after four years of laying track over marshes and streams, the first Shoreline train departed from New Haven, with stops at Fair Haven, Branford, Stony Creek, Guilford, Madison, Clinton and Westbrook before it arrived at Saybrook. In less than a month, there were two and, soon, three daily round trips that traveled between New Haven and New London in less than three hours. The train had to cross Connecticut River on the ferry *Shampishue* until a wooden bridge was built in 1870. That bridge was replaced by an iron one around 1907, and it remains today.

The railroad also brought manufacturing to Saybrook. In 1854, a joint stock company of residents was formed to manufacture skates, and a

Old Saybrook is on the main East Coast railroad artery. *Image courtesy of Old Saybrook Historical Society.*

building was constructed near the depot. However, after a few years, it went out of business, and the building was sold. The building stood idle for several years until it was bought and refurbished to serve as the St. John Roman Catholic Church. It served until a new church was constructed on Main Street in the 1930s.

There were many lines in the early days of railroading: The New Haven and Hartford joined with the New York and New Haven to form the New York, New Haven and Hartford in 1871. The company adopted an aggressive merger policy that eventually included over twenty-five lines, like the Shore Line Railroad, the New Haven and Northampton and the New York and Boston Air Line. Among the new lines that became part of the New Haven Line was the Connecticut Valley Railroad, which had its first run in 1871, from Hartford to Saybrook and then on to Saybrook Point and Fenwick.

With two routes coming together at what was then called Saybrook Junction, a station was needed to serve both lines. Part of the building faced the east–west tracks of the New Haven line and the other part faced the north–south track of the Valley Railroad. The Valley tracks ran at street level across today's parking lot, past Beard Lumber and then across spits of land, connected by small trestles around North Cove, to Saybrook Point. The New Haven line crossed Middlesex Turnpike, which was an extension of North Main Street, where a flagman controlled road traffic. Many years later, in 1966, Saybrook officials attempted to get the state highway department to construct a bridge over the tracks as a way to ease the traffic jams that were occurring where Route 1 and Route 9 met. The idea was rejected, and the traffic jams remain today.

A newspaper report dated September 2, 1874, noted:

> *The new Union depot at Saybrook Junction, and the two large freight depots, are fine buildings and much admired....The little octagonal brick*

building where the engines go "to take a drink" cost, with the well and fixtures, more than all the other buildings combined. In the top of this building is a huge water tank, with a capacity of 23,230 gallons and weighing when filled about 100 tons....A large locomotive drinks 1,800 gallons of water at a time, and about twenty of them are watered here every day....A curious little engine is stationed in the building, and it is kept very busy in drawing the water from the well nearby, carrying it up to the tank.

As the use of trains driven by steam engines increased, a reservoir was dug, and water was piped from high on the hills overlooking the Connecticut River to the tank at the junction. The reservoir remains, but the water that was used for steam power was replaced around 1950 by diesel power.

Passenger service between Hartford and Saybrook ended in 1933, and freight service from Middletown to Saybrook was abandoned in 1967. The track from Saybrook to Haddam was leased by railroad hobbyists who added vintage steam engines, cars and equipment and opened, in 1971, one hundred years after the opening of the Valley Railroad, the popular tourist attraction known as the Essex Steam Train and River Boat.

A switch tower was built about 1890 to keep the New Haven and Valley lines on separate tracks. However, the old tower was destroyed when a "runaway" boxcar crashed into the structure and killed the operator in 1912. A new tower was built and remained in operation until 1985, when the switching operations moved to Boston. Set in a V between the tracks of the two rail lines, the blue-gray building became the home of vagrants and pigeons and was offered at no charge to anyone who would move it. The State Historic Preservation Office offered to help, but there were no takers, and it was demolished.

During World War II, the station was very active, with long freight trains passing through, carrying tanks, trucks and guns with multiple steam engines. When Pratt Read was ordered to stop producing piano parts "for the duration," they made gliders, which were then packed in large wooden crates and shipped by train to Boston for transfer to Europe. Not much care was taken with the passenger station, and over the years, it deteriorated. In 1973, it was offered to the town, but the offer was not accepted. With the scruffy station and growing criticism of the rail line, a group of commuters and concerned residents, led by Dr. Wayne Southwick, a professor of orthopedic surgery at Yale and a resident of Old Lyme, organized the Shoreline Trains Association. First selectwoman Barbara J. Maynard formed an ad hoc committee to restore the station. Volunteers painted its exterior,

R. R. Station, Old Saybrook, Conn.

Saybrook served as a stop for the Connecticut Valley Railway, which connected with Hartford and extended south to Saybrook Point. *Image courtesy of Old Saybrook Historical Society.*

an Explorer Scout group cleaned the inside, the Shoreline Junior Women donated $2,000 to the project and even Amtrak contributed funds toward the station's improvement.

In 1984, Amtrak purchased 1.2 acres, which it combined with the station's existing 4.6 acres and placed the property up for bid to turn the area into an upscale development of stores and offices. They hoped to attract a drive-in bank and planned to establish a railroad museum. The new commercial area was designed by Halcyon Architects and constructed by Associated Development Corporation of Hartford, both from Hartford. The old freight building was moved in 1986 to the west side of the station, and it became a restaurant called O'Brannigan's; today, it is Pizzaworks. Amtrak maintains an office and supply room between the restaurant and the station. With uncertain schedules, poor service and run-down trains, the New Haven Railroad went bankrupt in 1961 and, after struggling for several years, was absorbed by the Penn Central in 1969. Penn Central was later absorbed into Amtrak, the national railway service that was created in 1971.

Aside from installing a new floor and at one time fresh but now fading paint, little was done to maintain the station. But between 2018 and 2020, the ancient mechanics were replaced, the structural deficiencies were remedied, other repairs were made and the building was painted. Most importantly, its historical integrity was respected.

A manual of regulations for railroad engineers from 1849 states, "One stroke of the bell signifies go ahead. Two strokes of the bell signify stop. Three strokes of the bell signify back." For the rail system today, it's not always clear how many times the bell has been stroked.

5

WRITERS AND FIGHTERS AT THE UPPER CEMETERY

*S*outh of where the railroad tracks slash through Old Saybrook, protected only by an iron fence, a narrow grass border and the road, is Old Saybrook's historic Upper Cemetery. This final resting place is partially enclosed by a stand of trees and shrubs that separate the graves from multiple apartment buildings and paved parking areas—a peaceful oasis in the midst of modern developments.

The cemetery's origins can be traced to at least May 27, 1786, when William Lynde, Travis Ayer and Joseph Willard were directed to survey the land and report about its use as a burial place. Sometimes called the Junction Cemetery or Municipal Cemetery, its 2.7 acres comprise the final resting places of forty-eight identified veterans from the French and Indian War, the American Revolution, the War of 1812 and the Civil War. The cemetery's first burial took place in 1787. The individuals buried there include many members of Saybrook's most prominent families: the Bushnells, the Whittleseys, the Clarkes, the Chalkers, the Spencers and others. The cemetery also contains the headstone memorializing "Fero, the faithful slave of William Lynde who died March 20, 1801, AGE 72 yrs." Travis Ayer, who served in the French and Indian Wars and was present at the siege of Louisbourg, Nova Scotia, and who helped plan the burial ground, was buried there in 1812.

According to Harriet Chapman Cheesebrough, who wrote *Glimpses of Saybrook in Colonial Days*, religious services were not conducted at burials during most of the colonial period. There was a last, often emotional, look at the remains as a mark of respect, she wrote, but there was no reading of scripture or prayer. A bell was tolled, and the coffin was placed in the ground. Afterward, refreshments were served at the house of the deceased.

Ms. Cheesebrough died in 1897 and was buried in the Upper Cemetery. The grave of Thomas Acton (1823–1898), the man for whom the library was named, can also be found in this cemetery. Acton took on the responsibility of courageously subduing the Civil War draft riots in New York City after the police commissioner was nearly beaten to death by angry mobs. He also contributed to the founding of the New York City Fire Department. A New York politician and reformer, Acton spent summers in his home near today's library on the Old Boston Post Road.

Many veterans from America's early wars are also interred at the Upper Cemetery. From the American Revolution: Moses Chalker (1759–1842), Sabeth Chapman Chalker (1768–1842), Oliver Chalker (1760–1846), William Waterhouse (unknown–1814), Captain Richard Sill (1722–1795), Captain Richard Still (1716–1795), William Parker (1761–1834), William Lord (1746–1825) and Elisha Chapman (unknown–1840). From the War of 1812: John Ayer (unknown–1840), William Beers (1794–1838), John Bushnell (unknown), Stephen Chalker (1792–1860), William Chalker (1773–1851), Joseph Fuller (1795–1832), David Ingham (1793–1820), Ezra C. Ingham (1792–1873), Stephen Ingham (1787–1840), Gilbert Kirtland (1793–1858), Anthony B. Ross (1769–1847), Elisha Sill (1772–1866) and John L. Whittlesey (1791–1870). From the Civil War: William Dawes (unknown–1910), George Dibble (1830–1863), Josiah Dibble (1830–1863), James Henry Harned (1840–1900) and Gilbert Hefflon (unknown–1864).

There is a possibility that there are unmarked graves outside the official boundaries of the graveyard, an area that was often reserved in the early colonial days for African Americans and Native Americans. This area was examined before apartment buildings were developed, and no evidence of burials was reportedly found.

The cemetery was maintained by the Upper Cemetery Association until 1956, when the group was disbanded, and its funds were turned over to the town. The grounds were neglected, and the gravestones deteriorated or were damaged and knocked over. Trees and invasive vegetation encroached on the perimeter, and the historic iron fence rusted and crumbled. Recognizing the need to restore the area, a committee composed of local residents was appointed in 1999 to take responsibility for the site. In 2002, the Upper Cemetery Association changed its name to the Municipal Cemetery Committee, and it began maintaining the site. The committee

This historic municipal cemetery has become an appreciated community site after years of neglect. *Image courtesy of Old Saybrook Historical Society.*

succeeded in cleaning and restoring the site and developing plans for its future; the committee's additions included a perpetual memorial garden to hold the remains of cremations. Local resident Scott Carson documented the cemetery's history and researched burial records, including probate records, genealogies, family records, correspondence, school records, wills, photos and other documents. From these records, Carson created the first detailed and comprehensive study documenting the Upper Cemetery and those buried there. The construction of the adjacent apartment buildings and reconstruction of North Main Street has improved the area, and the cemetery has received renewed interest and care.

James Crozier (1933–2004) was a navy veteran of the Korean conflict and an active chairman in the early 2000s of the Upper Cemetery Committee. He worked tirelessly to gather records and maintain and improve the cemetery. He and his wife, Jan, were among the last to be buried here.

6.

SAYBROOK'S MONKEY FARM

A local landmark with the curious name of the Monkey Farm Café has a long tradition of serving good food and plenty of drinks. Casual visitors wonder about its history and speculate about the origin of its unusual name. What better location could there be for a restaurant and hotel than a busy Main Street and Post Road intersection that's a short walk from the railroad station? That's probably what was going through the mind of young William Coulter of New York City. A frequent summer visitor in Old Saybrook since 1861, William attended school at the Seabury Institute on Main Street and finally moved to the town in 1884. In time, he married Mary Hefflon of Saybrook, and they had three children. Aside from causing the area's first automobile fatality when his car struck and killed Albert McQuestion in July 1904, Coulter was a distinguished citizen and a member of the local Masons and Elks.

The Coulter House had already been in the Coulter family for years when young William opened his hotel and began serving meals in 1892. At that time, the home was in an ideal location on the town green, not far from where Main Street crossed the ground-level railroad tracks. It was a favorite stopping place for traveling men who passed between the front of Coulter's building and the Whittlesey House (now Saybrook Home) on the road to the ferry. The hotel could accommodate thirty guests, and room and board went for a reasonable two dollars a day. Roast beef was a specialty, and a glass of whiskey could be had for ten cents. An early report stated:

The hotel furnishes good accommodation for its guests, the appointment of rooms, and the table service being equal to that of any country hotel. The location of the hotel being only two minutes' walk from the depot at Saybrook Junction, almost completely covered by large shade trees and only a short distance from the seashore makes it a very popular resort. There is a first-class café connected with the hotel and the traveling public may be sure of a most enjoyable place for rest and recreation should they visit the house, and most courteous treatment at the hands of Mr. Coulter and his efficient staff of assistants.

Coulter did well enough to add a livery stable. Guests arriving by rail could then have a good meal and a good night's rest and rent a horse or carriage to visit the area.

In May 1932, the hotel's new owner, Frank Steele, changed the name to the Old Saybrook Inn, and it specialized in serving New England turkey dinners. It remained the Old Saybrook Inn until 1968, when Harry Corning, who bartended there, and Tom Davies bought the building and business, including the dozen or more rooms on the second and third floors that housed single men of questionable means. The new owners ended the rooming business years ago, but they have not yet dealt with the early

Located on Route 1 and Main Street, this building was purchased by James Coulter in 1864 and has been used as an inn or restaurant ever since. *Image courtesy of Old Saybrook Historical Society.*

Head of Main and Ferry Sts., Old Saybrook, Conn.

Reasonably priced rooms, roast beef and strong whiskey made the Coulter House a favorite for traveling men. *Image courtesy of Old Saybrook Historical Society.*

bedsprings, chests, glassware and other distressed relics that are housed in rooms decorated by fading wallpaper and decades of dust. A wrinkled and stained guest book from the 1946–47 season lists guests from various locations in the United States and Canada, including two guests from Cornfield Lightship 118 and even a few from Main Street who perhaps needed a place to "sleep it off." Harry promoted local softball teams and, in the early 2000s, retired to Florida on a quest to improve his golf game. He left the business to his children, Dave, Deb and Laura.

There are many stories regarding the unusual name. Dave Corning said that it goes back to Ray Gallagher, a local fisherman and frequent customer who said, "Every time I come in here, there's a different monkey behind the bar." A slightly different story said the previous innkeeper occasionally over-indulged and, at those times, would throw the keys to a customer and say, "Watch the place 'til I get back, I'm going to the bank." He didn't mention the bank was in Reno and that he would be stopping off in Las Vegas for a few days. The customer shouted out to the crowd, "They'll let anyone work here, this place is nothing but a monkey farm!" And—proudly—it is.

7

REMEMBERING THE SACRIFICE

Since the end of World War II, it seems as if the U.S. military has been engaged in continuous warfare. But there was a time when the United States fought in a "war to end all wars." Often called the Great War, World War I has been remembered for its armistice, which took place on the eleventh day, of the eleventh month, at 11:00 a.m. In 1954, Armistice Day was renamed Veteran's Day, but it is still observed on November 11. The United States also honors veterans by observing Memorial Day on the last Monday in May. Both days honor American servicemen of all wars.

Memorial Day, originally known as Decoration Day, was established by General John Logan, a national commander of the Grand Army of the Republic. The holiday was first observed in 1868, when flowers were placed on the graves of soldiers at Arlington National Cemetery. The southern states continued to honor the Confederate dead until the end of World War I, when Memorial Day changed from honoring just those in the Civil War to those who died in all of America's wars. Today, Memorial Day is commonly a day for parades, but it is also a somber day of remembrance. Old veterans ride in convertibles, many Americans become a little teary-eyed and new flags are placed at gravesites. For some families, it is a day when their memories are a little sharper and their grief is a little deeper and sadder.

When the "war to end all wars" ended, the residents of many American towns wanted to commemorate the service of their sons and daughters. At

OLD SAYBROOK HONOUR ROLL

THEY PROCLAIM THE EVERLASTING CREED OF LIBERTY

This memorial to the veterans of World War I was later replaced by a granite monument that is on the town green today. *Image courtesy of Old Saybrook Historical Society.*

a town meeting in October 1925, the residents of Old Saybrook donated $1,000 to erect a memorial and place it on the small green in front of the old Coulter House (now the Monkey Farm). Eventually, the monument cost $1,925. The massive shaft of granite from a Barre, Vermont quarry was furnished by the McGovern Granite Company of Hartford, and the memorial was designed by New York City artist Franklin J. Naylor. The dedication ceremonies were held on the 150th anniversary of the signing of the Declaration of Independence, July 4, 1926.

A parade of members of the American Legion from adjoining towns was led by the Westbrook Band down Main Street. Boy Scouts and Camp Fire Girls escorted the two surviving veterans of the Civil War, Henry I. Clark and John Coulter, in an automobile. Selectman Frank S. Pratt acted as the master of ceremonies and introduced Reverend Edward M. Chapman, who offered a prayer. A flag was unfurled, and the large audience sang "The Star-Spangled Banner." The cover over the monument was then removed by Elizabeth Chapman, a Camp Fire Girl, and John Rathbun, a Boy Scout. Reverend Melville K. Bailey gave a brief talk about

In addition to the World War I monument, the town green has monuments to veterans of World War II, the Korean War and the Vietnam War. *Image courtesy of Old Saybrook Historical Society.*

the memorial and traced its beginnings to World War I, when the whole country was called on for support. He noted that the town always went over the top in Liberty Bonds and Red Cross drives.

The main address of the afternoon was given by Reverend J.R. Danforth of New London. He suggested that the monument represented the strong and rugged character of New England granite, the fathers who founded this colony and the American spirit of aspiration. The monument was to stand in honor of everyone from Saybrook who served their country and, in particular, the men who put their lives down in service of their country and all of humanity during the Great War. The Honor Roll lists Saybrook sons who served: forty-eight in the army, eighteen in the navy, nine in aviation and two in the Motor Transport Corps. Of these men, Henry Faulk was killed in action; he was the youngest son of Mr. and Mrs. Frederick Faulk of Saybrook Point. Harry enlisted in Company C of the 101st Machine Gun Battalion and was shipped overseas. He was twenty years old when he was killed on July 25, 1918. A well-attended memorial service was held at Grace Church. His body was finally returned home in September 1921, and he was buried at Cypress Cemetery.

With the realignment of Route 1 in the mid-1960s, it became necessary to relocate this war memorial to the town green on Main Street, where it joined a World War I cannon. Today, the old cannon is located at the local Veterans of Foreign Wars (VFW), and the town green has additional memorials commemorating the service of Old Saybrook's sons and daughters in other wars. Visitors should stop by, read the many names listed there and offer thanks for their service and sacrifice.

8.

MERCHANTS ORGANIZE

A momentous pivot in human history occurred between the late 1930s and 1941, when severe economic hardship gave way to all-encompassing military involvement. Small-town life went on as well as it could until the global troubles disrupted this everyday existence of ordinary families. Caught between the far edge of the Great Depression and the calamity of an oncoming world war, several Saybrook businessmen dealt with their economic issues by establishing a chamber of commerce.

After several years of economic depression, the shoreline and river valley economy began to stir in the late 1930s. The new Main Street movie theater had recently opened and featured *Gone with the Wind*. Frederick Sturgess III and Whitney Stueck bought the old power station and planned to operate it as a yacht yard. At Saybrook Point, the Pease House announced that it had sold a record-setting two thousand pounds of lobster during an August weekend. In Essex, the wealthy and well-connected Chester Bowles was back in port with his seventy-two-foot schooner after a worrisome six-day delayed return from Bermuda. Great technological progress occurred in Deep River, as dial phones arrived on April 1, 1938.

In 1939, a workman could earn $1,730 a year, and a typical house cost around $3,800, just a bit more than twice the average annual wage. An automobile cost around $700 and gas cost 10¢ a gallon. A pound of hamburger cost 14¢, and a loaf of bread cost 8¢. But ominous events were occurring around the world; Germany and the Soviet Union attacked Poland, and in September 1939, Britain, France and other Allied forces declared war on Germany. The United States decided to remain neutral, but in the same year, Albert Einstein, who frequently vacationed in Old Lyme and shopped in Old Saybrook, wrote President Franklin D. Roosevelt, urging him to initiate a program to develop an atomic bomb.

In this atmosphere, a meeting was held at the town hall on May 26, 1939, to launch an Old Saybrook Development Association. The group was formed in response to a letter from first selectman Gordon B. Smith. Seated around the table were state representative James U. Dibble and realtor George Kirtland, and they were listening to Oswald D. Quinlan of Meriden, whom they had invited to talk about creating a businessmen's organization. The group decided that they would get more information about forming a permanent organization and met again on June 2 to hear from the representatives of the Essex Board of Trade, the Old Lyme and Lyme Chambers of Commerce and the Westbrook Board of Trade. The group voted to organize an Old Saybrook Chamber of Commerce and adopted the Essex Board of Trade constitution, and a few weeks later, it elected the first officers of the organization.

Among the founding members was G. Fred King, the first elected president of the chamber who served from 1939 to 1942. He was the longtime office manager of the Southern New England Telephone Company office on Main Street and later served as Old Saybrook's first selectman from 1946 to 1955. He lived on Elm Street and had a summer cottage on Great Hammock Road. Dr. Aaron Greenberg, the organization's elected treasurer, was a highly esteemed family physician who lived in a stately home on Main Street, where he also operated his office from 1932 to 1983. He delivered most of the local babies for several generations and made house calls at any time—day or night. He served as a school physician and medical examiner and was instrumental in getting the town its first ambulance. The 1977 Town Report was dedicated to him, and it noted his "deep sense of devotion, concern, and love of people throughout his career, and his community is a better place because of him."

Fred LaMay, along with his brother Irving, established LaMay Brothers Garage and started the local Ford dealership, which is still in business today in the same location. Fred was elected to the chamber's board of directors. He served on the board of selectmen and the board of finance and was a volunteer member of the fire department. He was well known for playing baseball in the Middlesex County League and later coached and managed some of Saybrook's Little League teams. Irving LaMay founded the LaMay Construction Company in 1928 with a steam shovel

Among the leading businessmen was pharmacist Joseph Ranelli. His original pharmacy was on the corner of Main and Sheffield Streets. *Photograph courtesy of Linda Kinsella.*

he acquired from a customer who was unable to pay his bill. He was a member of the board of finance for twenty-three years and a chairman for fifteen years. In 1957, the *New Era* newspaper named him man of the year for his "distinguished public service to residents of Old Saybrook and the lower valley and shoreline communities."

A.L. Dudley was also a member of the first board of directors and a developer with real estate on Main Street. In 1928, he constructed the Dudley Building, which housed Saybrook Hardware and a variety of other stores. Dudley also owned Dudley's Dodge and Plymouth Garage across the street. In 1975, a room in the Historical Society's Hart House was dedicated to Albert Lawrence Dudley, noting, "He engaged in many mercantile pursuits, aided civic enterprises and influenced the development and character of our town."

Merle Patrick was also a member of the board of directors and was well known as the dean of merchants. He was the proprietor of Patrick's Country Store on Main Street from 1931 to 1971. There, he began selling dry goods and soon expanded his inventory to include "general merchandise," including clothing, shoes, cigarettes, newspapers and, especially, penny candy. He gave every child an ice cream cone at the end of the school year and every student with a good report card free root beer barrels, spearmint leaves and jawbreakers. Patrick rode his bike from his home on Lynde Street to work and everywhere else around town, and he always marched in the Memorial Day parade.

Gordon Smith, a member of the first board of directors, had a plumbing business in the store next to the old town hall, and it is now occupied by Esty's. He served as postmaster from 1928 to 1934 and was elected first selectman, an office that was also held by his father and, later, his son, Malcolm. Smith became the town's first fire chief in 1924, when the first company was housed in a small shed behind the town hall. His wife, Edith, served on the board of education.

Pauline Ward was noted for establishing, with her husband, the Saybrook Candy Company, which offered candies in silver-colored mahogany boxes and sweets in red-topped paper boxes. Ward and her husband, who helped preserve historical cemetery records, lived and ran the shop in a house on the corner of Main and Elm Streets that was originally purchased by her father before the stock market crash of 1929. During World War II, Ward worked for a defense contractor in Deep River and opened a real estate business. She became politically active and was an influential member of the Republican State Central Committee.

Other members of the early board of directors included:

- Egedio Baldoni, the chief mechanic at Saybrook Garage, which he and his brother John bought from the LaMays around 1946.
- Frank Brennan, the popular, always pleasant and generous proprietor of the famous Pease House.
- Joseph Cosulich, the town clerk for many years who sold real estate and developed the Knollwood Beach area, where he lived.

- Frederick Chapman, who had a fuel business with his brother and developed Indian Town. He lost his right arm in belted machinery in a sawmill, and when it was necessary, he drove by holding the steering wheel with his knee and leaning over to shift with his left arm.
- James Dibble, a state representative who managed the town road and maintenance crews when they mowed with a team of horses followed by a crew with scythes. His family remains in the construction business today.
- George Kirtland, who operated a real estate and insurance office on Main Street. He was known as a deal maker and impeccable dresser who was quietly called Beau Brummel.

Although they had already met several times, it was not until July 12, 1939, that the minutes recorded, "The first regular meeting of the Old Saybrook Chamber of Commerce was called to order at 8:30 p.m. by the president, Fred King, in the basement of the town hall." Not a lot of business was conducted, but the group did form a committee to recruit new businesspeople for the organization, and each member agreed to bring a guest to the next meeting who might join. Within a year, the group had attracted sixty-eight members.

Community issues received attention from the earliest members of the group. At the July 1939 meeting, the group voted to appoint a committee to "investigate and interest a bank to come into town." The group discussed the purchase of the Saybrook Point Wharf, the state establishment of the Saybrook Fort site, the dredging of North Cove, the unsatisfactory parking conditions on Main Street and the Christmas tree lighting. In a July 1939 article, the *New Era* newspaper supported the establishment of the chamber. It stated, "Old Saybrook is a real diamond in the rough. There is ample room in all directions for summer and year-round residences and a number of small industries. Not far from the center of the town, there is ample acreage for an airport of major size. City water is available on all the principal streets. Electricity and telephone service is everywhere."

Some of the issues that were discussed then are not too different from those that are discussed today. There was a "lengthy discussion," for example, on sanitation, and it was understood that it would soon become "compulsory to have septic tanks." Transportation issues also often caused concern, and frequent attempts were made to get the railroad to schedule stops in Old Saybrook. When Saybrook Bridge's automobile traffic was directed to Route 80, Saybrook joined

The Old Saybrook Chamber of Commerce is at the head of Main Street and also serves as a visitor information center. It moved here from farther south on Main Street in 2001, replacing a Mobil service station. *Photograph courtesy of the Old Saybrook Chamber of Commerce.*

with other shoreline towns to get the state highway commissioner to erect signs and maps to the scenic route along the coast. The chamber also discussed the possibility of having a seaplane base built at Saybrook Point.

There was always a complaint about how few residents attended the town meetings, because residents felt that everything was "cut and dried." The organization did successfully ask merchants to contribute toward the cost of printing a small booklet of facts which noted that Old Saybrook "has a rich heritage of historical charm, and its future possibilities as a community in which to work, live and play are tremendous." However, attendance began to drop in late 1941, and the minutes recorded that "only six members reported, so no business transacted," and "nothing of any importance discussed owing to small number present."

With growing numbers of young men going into armed service, factories converting to war work and the rationing of food, gas and everyday products, the total war effort impacted life as Saybrook's residents knew it. In September 1942, the chamber moved to only holding quarterly meetings, and then, no meetings were held until well after the war was over.

9

A PLACE CALLED SAYBROOK HOME

*O*ne of the oldest, largest and most-visited historic sites along Old Saybrook's shoreline is a place called Saybrook Home, or as the National Register of Historic Places identifies it, the Ambrose Whittlesey House. The house, now the centerpiece of a business that began in 1977 as the Marlboro Country Barn in Saybrook, had its origins in the farmland and forests where the original building, a one-story cottage, was constructed in 1765. A separate, two-story, gambrel-roofed structure was added to the home in 1799. Both sections are post-and-beam framed, sheathed with planking and clapboards and remain in use today. The main part of the house was built by Ambrose Whittlesey, a descendant of John Whittlesey, one of the early settlers in the area. John, along with his brother-in-law William Dudley, operated the ferry across the Connecticut River beginning in 1662, and the ferry was continuously run by the Whittleseys until 1839, when they conveyed it to the town.

Ambrose was born in 1761, in the family home, where the ferry departed from Tilley's Point, today's Ferry Road. Many of the Whittleseys were prosperous farmers, merchant traders and shipbuilders. When he turned twenty-one, Ambrose went to sea and eventually became a ship owner and a master of the schooners and sloops owned by General William Hart and the Griswolds of Old Lyme. He sailed to the West Indies, South America, Spain, Portugal and Northern Africa. He married Ann Waterhouse in 1783, and over the next several years, they had five sons and three daughters. He sailed on at least two long voyages. After leaving New London in 1803 on the brigantine *Sygnet*, Ambrose was bound for Surinam off the northeast coast of South America. On his return, he ran into a nor'easter off the coast of New Jersey that caused his ship to leak and eventually sink. Captain Whittlesey was reportedly washed overboard. He and his crew were later rescued by the ship *Polly* out of Kennebunk, Maine.

On another voyage, Ambrose commanded the ship *China* that was owned by the Griswold family of Old Lyme. After leaving New York Harbor in May 1822, he was bound for Lima, Peru; his plan was to sail around Cape Horn and up the west coast of South America. He reached Valparaiso, Chile, in October; Lima, Peru, in November; and from there, he sailed to Ecuador. His cargo included flour, wine, brandy, whiskey, chairs, tobacco and butter, and he returned with a cargo of copper, hemp and cocoa. The voyages were very profitable, but they were dangerous and required him to be away from home for long periods of time. Ambrose's voyage to the west coast of South America took nearly five months.

Aside from his life as a sea captain, Whittlesey served as a state representative for six terms between 1806 and 1818. Then, between 1820 and 1824, he returned to making long voyages, mostly to Spain and Portugal. He died in 1827 and willed the house to his youngest son, who was also named Ambrose; however, his widow continued to live there until she died in 1838. To obtain additional land, Ambrose Jr. (1803–1889) purchased two acres to add to his property. After his death, the property and building were passed to his daughter Elizabeth and remained in the family until 1967.

The home was last used as a private residence by Margaret "Peggy" and R. Linsley "Shep" Shepherd. Shep was friends with first selectman and historian Ros Whidden, and they researched old homes together. Later, Shep would go to his workshop in the old shed and make wooden identification signs to place on the houses built before 1850. Shep died in 1974, and Peg sold the house and property two years later to Clara and Carl Zirkenbach, the mother and stepfather of the home's current owner, Keith Bolles. Carl was the owner of Marlboro Country Barn, and Clara had opened a shop at Mystic Village that proved to be too small. Clara opened Marlboro Country Barn of Old Saybrook; its name was changed to Saybrook Country Barn in 1997, and it was changed again to Saybrook Home in 2019.

Soon after opening Marlboro Country Barn of Old Saybrook, Clara doubled the shop's original three thousand square feet. When the neighboring Saybrook Bank and Trust closed, she purchased a section of land behind her store from the bank and, in 1987, added a second and third barn to the rear of the original building. Just north of the Country Barn was a building

The additional development of this site has been sensitive to the house that was built in 1799 by sea captain Ambrose Whittlesey. *Photograph courtesy of Kasey Commander.*

owned by Earl Endrich, who ran his insurance agency in part of the building and rented another part to Cartier Optical. Whenever Keith Bolles, who by then was running the growing Country Barn, would see Earl, he would ask, "Earl, are you ready to sell the building?" Earl's answer was always, "No."

When driving by Earl's building on a snowy day in December 1997, Keith saw Earl, who had lost one arm, shoveling snow. He pulled alongside and again asked Earl if he was ready to sell. Earl paused, looked up and replied, "Damn right I am!" Keith parked his car right then and there, and the two went inside Earl's agency, wrote out an agreement and officially closed on the sale about a week later. The building could not be renovated, so it was replaced with reproductions that kept the Colonial flavor of the area.

The house next to Earl Endrich's building belonged to Bill Dawes, and he sold it to Country Barn in 1999. An additional house belonging to Jim and Jan Crozier was bought after Jim passed away in 2004. In 2007, additional barns were added, and an apparel shop and restaurant were opened. The original three-thousand-square-foot building had grown to a forty-two-thousand-square-foot complex that held bedroom sets, dining sets, assorted

This large complex maintains a historic flavor and is known as Saybrook Home. It offers fine furnishings, fashions and a restaurant. *Photograph courtesy of Kasey Commander.*

household items, clothing and a restaurant. Today, it attracts customers from throughout Connecticut, including the children and grandchildren of the first customers. Owner Keith Bolles maintains the barn's original historic features and has used its architectural style to grow his business. One can't help but think that knowing and appreciating history is good for business… and for Main Street and the community.

PAST POSTS

*A*fter drums and smoke, one of the great human achievements in communication has been writing messages on paper and delivering it. In fact, this method of connecting was so creative and useful that societies found ways to deliver messages to inhabitants both near and far. Younger readers may not realize this, but before mail appeared as text on a screen, people actually used hand-held writing devices applied to paper, and when they were done writing, that paper was folded or placed in an envelope and delivered, by courier, to its designated address. In colonial America, this arrangement led to the establishment of a mail service between New York and Boston in 1672, and two years later, it was expanded to Connecticut. Starting in 1813, mail was carried by steamboat; in 1832, by rail; in 1860, by pony; and in 1918, it was carried with a special stamp by air.

Early colonial messages were sometimes paid for by the person receiving the communication—but only sometimes. As any corporate consultant could see, this was not a good business model. A more workable system was established in 1775, when Benjamin Franklin was appointed postmaster general and eventually established a national mail system. By the late 1700s and into the first half of the 1800s, messages were written on a single sheet, folded, sealed with wax and given to a local postmaster who would collect a fee and sign the cover. Samuel Osgood, the first postmaster general in the newly formed United States, made an effort to bring some order and efficiency to the jumble of differing fees and established a system of prepaying a standard rate based on the distance the mail was sent (the fees started at six cents for 30 miles and went to a maximum of twenty-five cents for more than 450 miles).

Post roads were built and divided the landscape, but they provided connections between towns and cities. In 1802, a post road was carved from Middletown to the Haddams to Old Saybrook. By 1816, mail was being delivered weekly by a post rider on horseback. As the job grew in importance, the Middletown–Saybrook rider obtained a one-horse covered wagon and a fish horn to announce his arrival in town. Later, he added sleigh bells that he used all year. Friday was mail day, and his arrival was eagerly anticipated.

By the early 1830s, Connecticut had more than 2,500 miles of post roads and a scattering of markers and landmarks to help riders and stage drivers judge their distances and directions. Post offices were established fairly early in the shoreline towns: New Haven in 1790; Guilford in 1793; Killingworth (Clinton) in 1794; Pettipaug (Essex) in 1802; Branford in 1807; East Guilford (Madison) in 1814; West Brook in 1821; and Saybrook (Deep River) in 1828. The Old Saybrook Post Office was established on January 14, 1793, and the first postmaster's position was offered to General William Hart, who promptly declined the honor. Two weeks later, the position was offered to Humphrey Pratt Jr., who promptly accepted and served for thirty-five years until his son, Richard, took over.

Another post office was established in 1854 at Saybrook Ferry, with Elisha S. Howard serving as its first postmaster. The office was discontinued in 1864, reestablished in 1868 and discontinued again later that same year. In Fenwick (originally known as New Saybrook), the post office was located in the Dickinson and Kellogg Grocery Store, where Joseph Kellogg became the first postmaster in 1872. By the mid-1880s, Richard Dickinson ran the store and also served as postmaster. Mail to Saybrook Point improved in the 1870s, when the Connecticut Valley Railroad reached the town. When the rail service was discontinued, the post office established a "star route" that provided daily round trips by automobile to carry the mail between Middletown and Saybrook. The Saybrook Point Post Office finally closed in 1956.

Early post offices were often kept in general stores and grocery stores, where they generated extra income and attracted new customers. Not surprisingly, many proprietors became postmasters. In those days, before civil service, postmasters generally obtained their positions through political appointment and were removed when administrations changed. At the Goodspeed Opera House Post Office, Republican Marshall Emmons and Democrat James Bridges overcame this job insecurity by appointing each other as their assistant every time administrations changed, and they became the new postmaster.

There was some confusion in 1902, when Saybrook Republicans recommended twenty-six-year-old J.A. Ayer for the postmaster position, and the appointment went, quite unexpectedly, to J.A. Sangle. It turned out that J.A. Sangle and J.A. Ayer were the same person. Ayer's father was Adam Sangle, who died a short time after J.A. was born, and J.A.'s mother remarried Andrew Ayer. While her son adopted Ayer as his name, no legal steps were ever taken to change it, so his legal name remained Sangle. John A. Ayer ran the post office in the early 1900s from his shoe store on the Old Boston Post Road (today, the store is a dance studio). The post office remained there until 1929, when the newly appointed postmaster, Gordon Smith, added the office to his plumbing shop next to the town hall on Main Street.

Smith remained postmaster until he was succeeded in 1934 by Edward Bowes, who received rave reviews for his new equipment, large public space and for being located in "the heart of the business section of the town." However, by 1938, the U.S. Postal Service was looking for a new and larger facility with updated equipment, and when the bid to construct a new office was won by Leo Bonoff of Madison, Gordon Smith and many others in town cried foul. Smith, who was a respected and highly influential Republican in town—and, since 1934, the first selectman—claimed to have submitted a bid, showing improvements in equipment, which were requested by the post office department. The newspaper reported "a strong feeling of dissatisfaction" was felt among businessmen about the proposed change, and they felt they would be inconvenienced.

Thomas J. Curran Jr., the chairman of the local Democratic Party, also voiced disapproval, saying, "It seems very unfair that the post office should be moved with no conversation given those patrons whom the office serves." Curran encouraged people to write to postmaster general James A. Farley to express their opposition to the plan. The townspeople belatedly attempted to introduce a protest resolution at a town meeting; they threatened legal action, and Curran wrote to Senator Francis Maloney to investigate. But the decision had been made, and the new post office was built and opened next to the theater.

When postmaster Edward Bowes died in 1943, Thomas Curran Jr. was appointed to the position to complete his term. Curran went on to have a long and distinguished career that included the huge transformation that occurred after R.R. Donnelley, the printers of more than a million weekly

SAYBROOK THEATRE AND U.S. POST OFFICE, SAYBROOK, CONN.

Above: Additions were built in the late 1930s on either side of the theater to accommodate retail shops and a new post office. *Image courtesy of Old Saybrook Historical Society.*

Left: This building was used for a short time as a post office and has since housed medical and business offices. A larger post office was constructed across the street. *Image courtesy of Old Saybrook Historical Society.*

Life and *Time* magazines, came to town. The office next to the theater served as the post office through the postwar years, but the growing community needed a larger facility, and a new brick office was constructed and opened in 1957 at 51 Main Street. Then, once again, growing needs prompted the post office to construct another facility, this time across the street; this is the post office that exists today. The new building was officially opened by first selectman Raymond Kolowski on June 3, 1972, with Tom Curran's brother-in-law Elton F. Deckelman as postmaster.

Today, with the assorted services offered by Google, Facebook, Apple and other companies, you may find that the greatest impact comes from receiving a written message that has been personally delivered. So, send a letter or postcard to someone today.

II

MUSKETS ON MAIN

*M*ain Street kicks into high gear on a Saturday evening in December, when Old Saybrook's Torchlight Parade combines the sound of muskets with songs being sung on the town green. The local torches have been passed since 1971, but the tradition has roots deep in the English colonial period, when a day was set aside annually for citizen soldiers to be mustered, or called in, for training and to make sure they had a weapon. Each town had its own military company, and the selectmen were responsible for ensuring that there was enough firepower to defend the people and their homes.

After brief and disorganized drills and maneuvers on the town green, the rest of the day was spent socializing and making merriment. This often included an ample supply of rum that was provided by commanders seeking to win the favor of their men. Music was provided by fife and drum corps; both are ancient instruments that were used by armies to relay orders to soldiers in camp or in battle. The beat and rhythm of the drum, with the high, shrill pitch of the fife, carries well and keeps soldiers' minds from dwelling too much on the unpleasant conditions and tedious marches of war. Fife and drum corps disappeared from the military after the Civil War, and today, the only remaining corps is the Old Guard Fife and Drum Corps that is attached to the Third U.S. Infantry Regiment, a ceremonial army unit based in Fort Myer, Virginia.

While muster day and fifes and drums have disappeared from the military, the spirit of the tradition lives on in Old Saybrook and its annual Torchlight

Parade. The town's tradition began in 1971, when the Colonial Saybrook Fife and Drum Corps, under the direction of Bill Reid, revived the village muster as a salute to the ancient fife and drum corps and colonial militias. Bill Reid was one of the first paid police officers in the town, but his passion was music and military history. He collected enough military items to open a museum in Westbrook, and he had a number of military vehicles that he used to take his grandsons camping. He created the Old Saybrook Fife and Drum Corps in the early 1970s, and he went on to organize and host the first Christmas Torchlight Parade.

Modern revelers, with thoughts of a cold winter parade, may be surprised to learn that the original event was a two-day program held in June. Modeled after the pattern of a military ceremony known as a tattoo, from the Dutch word *tiptoe* that means to close the tops (of kegs), it was originally a drum beat played to inform tavern keepers that it was time to close their bars and for soldiers to return to their quarters. After an evening torchlight parade, retreat ceremonies would be performed by the sailing masters of the 1812 Essex Fife and Drum Corps. Then, the Liberty Tree historian from South Weymouth, Massachusetts, accompanied by the Third Connecticut Regiment from Glastonbury, raised a liberty pole. This was followed by music from several corps and, as the program described it, "jollification." The evening ended with the playing of "Taps."

The Torchlight Parade began as a daytime tattoo during the summer. Today, it is a popular December evening event. *Photograph courtesy of Ken Reid.*

A grand muster parade stepped off the following day at noon. Dignitaries from the political and musical world, led by Old Saybrook first selectman Jesse Johnson, lined the reviewing stand. There were around thirty music groups, including those from Old Sturbridge Village and several from New Jersey, Brooklyn, the Bronx, Greenwich and Rhode Island. A group of youngsters from Williamsburg, Virginia, who had formed a Civil War

Opposite: The event draws dozens of fife and drum corps and thousands of visitors to Main Street. *Photograph courtesy of Ken Reid.*

Above: The parade concludes with holiday songs at the town green. *Photograph courtesy of Ken Reid.*

fife and drum corps and researched and carefully made their Confederate uniforms, were the featured corps.

The following year, the Torchlight Parade was moved to early December, the time of year that was traditionally used by New England colonial militia for their muster; a number of Santas and the festive holiday spirit increased the "jollification." Each year, several thousand people join the festivities by donning foolish Santa caps and long johns and, perhaps, ingesting something to keep warm. The largest audience was recorded when the town celebrated its 350th anniversary in 1985. Music groups from as far away as Maine and Virginia participated in the parade. Police chief Edmund Mosca estimated the crowd at ten thousand. That year, the throng arrived at the newly completed gazebo on the town green for the community sing that was led by Old Saybrook music director John Torrenti, as it had been for many years. One participant recalled that a gentle snow began to fall as the crowd sang

"Silent Night." When the crowd finished the last verse, somewhat amazed by Mother Nature's timing, they all applauded.

Following a historic tradition, today's militia marches in its colonial-style regalia to the town green. Leading the gala event are the town's selectmen, in colonial dress, followed by dozens of fife and drum corps and other musical groups, scouts, school music groups and an assortment of floats. The young and old follow, carrying torches, lanterns and thermoses. Gathering at the town green, the village militia and civilians are warmed with hot chocolate, blankets and sometimes brandy as they enjoy the excitement of the season.

12

LADIES OF THE CLUB

A group of green-thumb gardeners who started meeting in the mid-twentieth century, wearing white gloves and drinking tea served in fine china grew to become the Garden Club. The club's primary purpose was, and remains, civic beautification, but members also work to stimulate interest in horticulture, promote conservation of natural resources and educate the community by encouraging projects and programs that focus on gardening. Founded by a dozen women at a meeting in the home of Mrs. Allen Talcott on August 11, 1952, the Old Saybrook Garden Club has become best known for maintaining twenty-three cheerful garden spots on Main Street's median dividers, but it does much more.

The club's membership in its early days, as it is today, was composed of several newcomers who were interested in cultivating plants and making new friends while promoting the beautification of their adopted community. It made sense—transplants seeking new roots establish a garden club. The club began hosting annual flower shows and monthly meetings in members' homes, a practice that continued until it moved to more public facilities. The club's first civic projects were to plant window boxes at the railroad station and a Christmas tree on the town hall lawn. The club planted bulbs and dogwoods at the new Goodwin Elementary School and at the Acton Public Library. At the library, the club also donated books and began providing desktop floral arrangements, a practice that continues today with fresh arrangements throughout the year.

By the late 1950s, the club was asked to supply plants for the wooden tubs that lined the narrow divider down Main Street. Soon, red and white petunias, geraniums, ivy and other plants graced the roadway. When the tubs deteriorated in 1971, they were replaced by half-barrels that were contributed by the A.R.C. Construction Company and painted by the Exchange Club. Flowers once again bloomed on Main Street. For the nation's bicentennial in 1976, the blue and white barrels were planted with red geraniums and white alyssum for a colorful and patriotic display.

However attractive the barrels, the Main Street median strip was a narrow and unsightly disfigurement that stretched from the Post Road to the town hall. Through the efforts of several civic organizations, separate and well-defined islands with small plots of land for plantings replaced the strip in 1995. Each spring, the Garden Club chooses a color scheme, and individual members plant and care for the twenty-three island spaces. At the end of the growing season, before Thanksgiving, members place forty-six lighted Christmas trees in the planters and forty-six wreaths on the lamp posts. The first trees were made from upside-down tomato cages with garlands and lights that wound from the wide bottom up the narrower rungs to the top. At the head of Main Street, in front of Saybrook Home, the members of the Garden Club created and still maintain the Constitution Garden. They also care for the flower bed in front of the fire station and the planters at the library.

As a special project, member Judy Grover saved and nursed seedlings from the town's remaining centennial elms. These trees were first planted in 1876 to honor the nation's founding, but most of them were lost to storms and elm disease. An example of this second-generation growth is now thriving on the town hall green. All members work on projects. If they've been in the club for ten years or so and find that they cannot give 100 percent, they become associate members and work when they can. Proving that meaningful work provides its own satisfaction, the club has several longtime members, and its turnover rate is very small.

Former first selectwoman Barbara J. Maynard holds top honors for being the longest-serving member of the Garden Club, having joined in 1957. She said that she simply joined because she liked gardening and liked to decorate. Her grandmother was a great gardener, and Maynard suspects she inherited it. "It is a very hardworking group," one member said. "We don't sit around. Members are committed." With one exception, there have been no male members, although there is nothing stopping them from joining, and many husbands who drive pickup trucks, haul equipment and do

Each year, the Garden Club conducts major projects on Main Street and elsewhere and raises funds with a plant sale. *Image courtesy of Old Saybrook Historical Society.*

The median divider, with planters and gas lights, was installed with volunteer labor in 1995 to beautify Main Street. *Image courtesy of Old Saybrook Historical Society.*

other chores may feel an especially strong connection to the group. George Maynard often came along to help his wife, Barbara, and others. He drove a truck, moved furniture, put up tables and pitched in to help in many ways. In the early 1980s, Garden Club president Jan Fenger presented George with a small gold-painted shovel and honorary membership. Not one to rest on his honors, George continued to help for many years with his shovel and truck.

To pay for its many activities, the club sponsors one fundraiser each year that is announced with the appearance of more than a dozen decorated bicycles around town. The annual Gardener's Market is held under a large white tent on the town green on Main Street on the Friday and Saturday before Mother's Day. There, one can find annuals, perennials, shrubs, herbs, vegetables and selections of plants dug from members' own gardens. There is also a tag sale, a bake sale and a children's activity area at the market. Profits from the market go to pay for the Main Street median plantings, holiday decorations, the Constitution Garden at the head of Main Street, the Street Garden Recognition Program, a college scholarship, the Sprouts educational program at Goodwin Elementary School, the flower arrangements and flower boxes around Acton Library, the flower bed in front of the fire station, high school graduation flower arrangements and expenses for other activities. So, when you're on Main Street, take some time to smell the roses, and say thanks to those ladies with their dirty knees, soiled hands and heads in the sun—they make Main Street blossom.

13

THE VALUE OF PENNY CANDY

A generation or two ago, when many local people owned and ran local shops, they were part of the fabric of the community and provided more than goods and services to young customers. Shopping was a bit more personal, and a child with a few coins could enter a favored shop, survey the wares and make a choice. To conduct this type of independent research and decision-making, there was no place quite like Patrick's Country Store.

By all accounts, the store's proprietor, Merle Patrick (1891–1977), got what he gave: love and respect, fairness and friendship, courtesy and care and untold lessons on living. He knew that there was no such thing as a small act of kindness; every act, like a pebble in a still pond, rippled to unknown shores. For forty years, the down-east Yankee, Old Saybrook's dean of merchants, the soft-spoken, good-natured, warm-hearted proprietor of Patrick's Country Store, represented the best of what is now a bygone era.

Merle Patrick was the fourth of five children born to Lewis and Elizabeth Patrick in Gorham, Maine. As a young man, he worked six days a week in a Portland music store as a clerk and salesman. He earned $6.00 a week but spent $1.50 of it on the daily train trip between Gorham and Portland. He was inducted into the army in 1917, and he was stationed with his unit at St. Pierre, outside of Tours, France, where he served for eighteen months as a bugler in the 303rd Regiment of the 76th Division Infantry. He was honorably discharged in 1919.

Shown here are leading Main Street merchants Joe Ranelli, Merle Patrick and Herbert Stokes. *Image courtesy of Old Saybrook Historical Society.*

He married his hometown sweetheart, Aravesta Sanford, in 1914, and after he was discharged from the army, he and "Vesta" lived in Essex, Connecticut, where he ran a store for his brother-in-law, Ernest Libby. The couple's daughter, Geraldine, was born in 1919, and their son, Wayne, was born in 1925. By the late 1920s, Merle and Vesta moved to Old Saybrook, where they rented a house on Pennywise Lane. When Wayne was ten years old, Merle bought him an Imperial bike for his birthday so that he could get to school. It is not certain how often Wayne used that bike, but it is clear that Merle used it regularly. Although Merle got his driver's license in 1922, he never owned a car, and aside from a few times that he used Ernest's car between Essex and Saybrook, his preferred method of travel was that bike, which he pedaled everywhere, at all times of the year, for the rest of his life.

This area was the center of town activity, with the Economy Market, the Gilt Edge Hamburger and Soda Shop, a pool parlor, the Stokes Store and the town's first gas pumps. *Image courtesy of Old Saybrook Historical Society.*

On March 6, 1931, with the Great Depression on the country's doorstep, Merle Patrick opened a stationery and apparel shop at 288 Main Street in Old Saybrook. It had a dim interior, a tin ceiling, a nest of cubbyholes for customer newspapers and wood-framed glass display cases. Fred Beebe ran an electrical appliance business next door, and Stokes Brothers Grocery and Joseph Ranelli's Drug Store were close by.

Patrick's carried shoes, men's furnishings, sporting goods, school supplies, hardware, comic books and penny candy. Every weekday after school, the place was overflowing with youngsters from the nearby elementary school who were stopping by to make candy selections. With a little brown bag in one hand and a candy scoop in the other, Merle would wait for the momentous decision: spearmint leaves, chocolate babies, jaw breakers, licorice sticks or root beer barrels. With just a few pennies and so many possibilities, it would sometimes take a while for customers to make a decision, but Merle waited ever patiently for them. His store was also the place where children could find brown-and-white saddle shoes for school. His customers also purchased notebooks and pencils, coloring books, games, puzzles, yo-yos and harmonicas. At Halloween, Patrick's was the place to buy a mask and costume. During Christmas and other holidays, the place was decorated.

Mostly, however, as one once young customer remembered, "Sometimes, I would just go visit and have a friendly chat. He never once seemed to get tired of me. There were always children going in and out for no reason; he had a cordial greeting for them all." Many Saybrook residents have lifelong memories of their last days of school, when Merle would send lollipops for every student in the school. "Then, we would all flock to his store to thank him," said one former student. "We knew that he would never forget us—and this was his way of letting us know that he was thinking of us."

Merle helped raise two generations of Old Saybrook youngsters. Once in a while, one mother recalled, "I would visit the store with my boys. I could look back into the past and see myself standing where they now stood, peering into the same old candy case." She watched her children, with their wide eyes gleaming, struggling to decide what to buy; they would then make their decision, satisfied enough to leave the store with a little brown bag in their tiny hands. She knew they were developing a long-lasting friendship with the little man behind the counter.

Merle was a selectman in the late 1930s and early 1940s, and he served as the first selectman for eighteen months to fill the unexpired term of Gordon Smith, who had died in office. He was a founder of the local chamber of commerce and belonged to the American Legion for more than fifty years. Three days before he turned eighty in 1971, after growing to be a frail, bespectacled little man with a high-pitched voice, Merle sold the store to Robert and Betty Van Zandt. He retired to the front porch of his house on Lynde Street.

The Van Zandts upgraded some of the store's products and maintained the same atmosphere until 1985, when they sold the store to Barry Maynard, who also kept the Merle Patrick name and atmosphere. But the mom-and-pop shops on Main Street were losing customers to national chains in large malls. Patrick's Country Store closed for good in 1999. When it did, many lost more than penny candy.

14

MUSIC AND DRAMA ON MAIN

*T*he former town hall and theater were built in 1910 and 1911 to house municipal offices and to provide a theater for dramatic and musical presentations and an auditorium for community gatherings. The imposing, two-story red brick building was constructed in the business district on Main Street. The Colonial Revival–style building was designed by New London architect James Sweeney and served as a town hall and a theater. Its original entrance was an imposing flight of stairs framed by two-story-tall Doric columns. Constructed with widespread community support, this was the first building owned by the town for municipal purposes, and it housed government offices from 1911 to 2004. At that time, it became the Katharine Hepburn Cultural Arts Center.

In the early days, there was only a limited need for town offices, and the space was easily divided to include meeting rooms and a jail cell. Vaults were located in the center of the building, and they were used as the town clerk's office. Partitions provided space for the fire marshal, tax assessor, registrar of voters and several other town officials. The idea for the new town hall came from Joseph A. Cone (1868–1918), a civic-minded printer, poet and writer who was best known for his humorous pieces. The Old Saybrook Musical and Dramatic Club was founded in 1905 at a meeting at Cone's home, and it was incorporated in the following years by Cone, Benjamin H. Chalker, Irwin Granniss, Calvin C. Fairbank, John S. Dickinson and Frank S. Pratt. The purpose of the club was to provide "a building suitable for town and social purposes." To raise funds, the club gave plays and concerts and hosted

TOWN HALL, SAYBROOK, CONN.

At a town meeting, residents unanimously approved the expenditure of nearly $50,000 to construct the new town hall. *Image courtesy of Old Saybrook Historical Society.*

suppers, and on January 8, 1908, the club purchased land next to the graded school on Main Street.

At the June 8, 1909 club meeting, the members unanimously voted to turn the organization's property and money raised for the purpose of constructing a town hall over to the town on condition that it appropriate the remainder of the money needed to construct a building. That was done with an appropriation of $5,000 and the appointment of a building committee. The following year, William L. Roe Jr. of New London began construction of the building, and it was dedicated in 1911. By January 1908, the young corporation had raised enough money to purchase land, and three and a half years later, its dream was realized with the opening of the Old Saybrook Town Hall on Main Street. The Deep River *New Era* called the new building "a substantial and artistic piece of architecture…a worthy addition to our beautiful Main Street."

The first performance in the new building was a drama called *Wedding Bells*, and it was presented by the Ivoryton Dramatic Club. Aside from serving as home for the Musical and Dramatic Club, the town hall screened the first movies in Old Saybrook, served as a basketball court for the school and gave shelter to the Ivoryton Players when World War II made their remote playhouse too difficult to reach. Theatrical performances, concerts, high school graduations, dances, banquets and other forms of entertainment were all presented in the building. The Musical and Dramatic Club continued to operate until 1935, when it contributed its remaining funds to the town to pay for improvements and a grandstand for the baseball field.

The town's government was centralized in this building; renovations were made in the 1950s, and the building continued to be used as a town hall until the town offices were moved to the adjacent former school building. Town residents voted to approve use of the former town hall as the Katharine Hepburn Cultural Arts Center in 2004. Over the years, as Katharine Hepburn became Kate and she built international fame as an actress, the building became an integral part of Main Street and the Saybrook community. Katharine Hepburn reached stardom but always came back to Old Saybrook and her home in Fenwick. It was a place she called paradise, and it was to this paradise that she retired in 1997, sixty-five years after her big-screen debut. That same year, with the town offices in the new town hall, the residents of Old Saybrook voted to restore Mr. Cone's building to its original use as a theater. Two years later, the theater was named the Katharine Hepburn Cultural Arts Center.

In recent times, the Kate has presented over 250 performances a year, including everything from ballet and magic to music and dance.

Programs at "the Kate" are a major attraction for visitors to Main Street. The building also houses a small museum of Hepburn artifacts. *Image courtesy of Old Saybrook Historical Society.*

In addition, the Kate offers a children's performance series each season, and it provides opportunities for young area thespians to perform. Each summer, the Kate hosts Kate's Camp for Kids, a weeklong intensive program that introduces children to the performing arts. Along with its live performances, the Kate shows simulcasts from the National Theatre of London, the Metropolitan Opera and the Bolshoi Ballet of Russia. It has partnered with Connecticut Public Television on a national series affectionately called *The Kate*. And, oh yes, from time to time it offers vintage movies starring "the great Kate."

Note: This essay is based on material originally published by the Katharine Hepburn Cultural Arts Center and the National Register of Historic Places.

15

STREET "PEDALERS"

*I*magine an economical, non-polluting, energy-efficient, fat-fighting, health-improving machine that advances technology, encourages paved roads, promotes women's rights and even has a bell that goes "ding dong." Now, imagine it was a few years ago and this self-powered machine had two fat tires of the same size and is the highly desirable machine called a *safety*. Fast-forward to Saybrook-by-the-Sea at the turn of the twentieth century. A sour note describes the place in dreamy terms:

> [Saybrook] *has no manufactures, no special industries, no anything— just itself.... There are a few little stores that blink sleepily at the passerby with half open shutters and to the uninitiated it is not apparent how the inhabitants make a living... The main occupation seems to be riding about in buggies or on bicycles. In this one thing, Saybrook is quite up to date; she has bicycles both epidemic and chronic and the only sound which startles the brooding stillness is the ding dong of the four inch gong which heralds nearly every bicycle. The two main streets are beautifully macadamized with trap rock, crushed fine, affording a hard even gray colored roadbed, a joy forever to wheelmen.*

Until the 1860s, people traveled by coach, horseback or by walking. At that time, a very uncomfortable, pedal-powered velocipede, often called a "boneshaker," for obvious reasons, was developed in France and introduced to the United States. For the first time in America, at the Weed

Sewing Machine Company in Hartford, sixty-inch "high-wheelers" were manufactured by the Columbia Bicycle Company. These expensive, high-wheeled ordinaries provided the unprecedented exhilaration of speed and the freedom of far-ranging mobility, but they were limited to the adventurous and wealthy—they were not for ordinary people.

That all changed in the mid-1880s, with the introduction of an improved machine that had two identically sized wheels and a chain drive. Called the safety, this machine was the forerunner of today's bicycle. Within a few years, there were more than three hundred American wheeler-dealers producing more than one million bicycles each year. The safety helped bring about the biking craze of the 1890s and helped change women's fashions and attitudes. The "new woman" challenged conventional Victorian wisdom by working outside of the home, becoming politically active and seeing herself as equal to men. For women, replacing tight corsets and hazardous long dresses with trousers and short covering dresses, called bloomers, provided them with a sense of freedom. Women's rights advocate Susan B. Anthony is widely quoted as saying, "Let me tell you what I think of bicycling. I think it has done more to emancipate women than anything else in the world. It gives women a feeling of freedom and self-reliance. I stand and rejoice every time I see a woman ride by on a wheel…the picture of free, untrammeled womanhood."

Along the shoreline, the *New Era* newspaper reported in July 1888, "The bicycle fever seems to have struck Saybrook bad. New machines and secondhand ones are constantly being brought here, and before long, they will be as plenty as horses." The newspaper was soon reporting, "The Ivoryton Bicycle Club came down Saturday night and enjoyed one of the Pease House famous suppers. The boys presented a fine appearance as they rode though the principle streets." In April 1891, the newspaper noted, "Many of the bicycles owned in town have been equipped with bells, a much-needed improvement, especially appreciated by pedestrians."

There were also more fundamental improvements that contributed to cycling enthusiasm, including the air-filled rubber tires that were invented by John Boyd Dunlop in 1888. One of the more significant snags to cycling, especially in areas outside the cities, were rutted dirt roads that were dusty when dry and muddy when wet. That all began to change when the newly formed League of American Wheelmen began agitating for improved roads. This Good Roads Movement led states, for the first time, to significantly participate in road building projects, and it later paved the way, as the biking craze gave way to the coming of the automobile. By the early 1900s, prominent publications were reporting that, in Saybrook, "the roads are perfect. The way from the [Main Street] junction to the Point is macadamized and as 'smooth as a floor.' The town is at present putting in a macadam bed on the road toward Essex."

Perhaps not surprisingly, some bicycles were wrongfully pedaled away without the owner's knowledge or permission. "Bicycle thieves have been getting in their work the past week in this place," said a newspaper report in 1904. "Two wheels having been stolen from in front of houses and, as yet, no trace has been found of either." The report stated one "wheel" was taken from a home on Main Street, "and last evening, a wheel belonging to E.L. Pollock, purchasing agent of the N.Y., N.H. & H. railroad was stolen from in front of the summer residence of ex-governor Buckley at Fenwick, where Mr. Pollock was calling."

Several bike shops existed in the area and later became automobile shops, and in Bridgeport and New Britain in particular, there were shops with tinkerers who had wild ideas about traveling above ground. In Saybrook, Spencer's Cycle Shop opened in a shed purchased by Dan Spencer on the Old Post Road near the bridge over the Oyster River. In 1907, the fancy publication *American Suburbs* noted that John F. Coulter repaired bicycles and automobiles and also did light machine work. "Mr. Coulter has a well-established reputation as a reliable dealer and repairer, and he gives prompt attention to all orders....He sells all the leading makes of wheels at the lowest prices, and he carries a full line of the latest models. He also offers bargains in secondhand wheels all in good repair."

Saybrook remains quite up to date as an attraction for people riding about on bicycles, and there are more occupations than riding about in buggies or on bicycles and considerably more sounds that "startle the brooding stillness" than "ding dong."

16.

SPARE TIME

To walk into a bowling alley some time ago was to enter a light-deprived, cigar-scented, noisy cavern, where slim bodies in satin shirts whipped small balls down narrow, highly polished alleys to distant forests of bruised white pins. They were also gathering places, where teams of company men engaged in friendly competitions and where boys could set pins and quickly earn, well, "pin" money.

Bowling has a long-lived and entrenched place in our culture. Unfortunately, it began with an unsavory reputation stemming from Puritan attitudes condemning all things pleasurable as being harmful to morality. Its acceptance increased with the invention of the lawn mower by Edwin Beard Budding in 1830, which provided maintenance of outdoor bowling greens.

The most notable bowling event in literature can probably be found in Washington Irving's story of Rip Van Winkle, who was awakened from a twenty-year slumber in the New York Catskills by the crash of ninepins. Many wealthy industrialists included lanes in their mansions, and the oldest surviving bowling lanes in the United States can be found in Roseland Cottage, which was built in 1846 in Woodstock, Connecticut, as the summer estate of Henry C. Bowen. However, bowling became a magnet for gambling, and in 1841, Connecticut made it illegal to maintain any ninepin lanes. But by the 1890s, tenpin bowling was permitted and popular.

Initially, ball weights and pin dimensions varied, and a major step toward standardization took place at a meeting that was organized by Joe

Thum at Beethoven Hall in New York City on September 9, 1895. There, representatives from America's bowling clubs established the American Bowling Congress. The game continued to grow in popularity, and by the early 1900s, the Brunswick-Balke-Collender Company of New York introduced the sixteen-pound, twenty-seven-inch-circumference tenpin ball known as the Mineralite. The company offered other supplies and equipment, including maple, kiln-dried tenpins, duck and candle pins and a partly automatic pin setter—although it still required pin boys to load the machine. With a truly automatic pinsetter, the popularity and number of bowling alleys increased in the 1950s and 1960s, and even before then, leagues of bowling teams had established competitive weekly schedules. Contributing to the popularity of the game was programming on network television, including *Championship Bowling*, *Make That Spare*, *Celebrity Bowling*, *Bowling for Dollars* and broadcasts of pro bowler championships.

The earliest bowling alley in Saybrook was located on Main Street, just north of what was Fiorelli's Furniture Store. Its existence is fondly remembered. When it was opened and how it closed seems shrouded in uncertainty, but it was a popular area attraction from the end of World War II to the early 1960s.

Several industrial leagues met there weekly, over a roughly thirty-week season. Five-member teams played three games, and their scores were totaled

The bowling alley was an inviting place for many residents to spend time and for youngsters to earn spending money by setting pins. *Image courtesy of Old Saybrook Historical Society.*

to determine the winning team and their standing in the league. At the end of the season, the winning team and outstanding individual scorers would often receive a trophy at a banquet that was held at the Casino Grill on the Boston Post Road or some other distinguished establishment. The Lower Middlesex County Industrial Bowling League, for example, included Pratt Read from Deep River, the Connecticut Light and Power working crew based in Essex, the workers who made electric motors and timers at Cramers in Essex, the Saybrook Laundry workers, the Bates knitting needle workers from Chester, the Essex lamp shade shop Verplex, lamp makers at Sight Light in Essex and other factory teams. Among the league's consistently leading high scorers were Walt Lindner of Deep River and Steve Witkowski of Cromwell. Some of the high rollers on the Saybrook team included Paul Solari, who worked for Ponds; Jim Fillmore, who worked at the telephone company; and Johnny Grief, who worked at the post office.

For a time, the alleys were owned and run by Frank Ferrari, who lived in Deep River and worked full time at Pratt Read. It was not unusual to sometimes find him sleeping at his desk late at night in the bowling alley. After World War II, he would arrive at the alley in his Kaiser Fraser automobile. In addition to the alley's six- and eight-paired bowling lanes, there were two pool tables that could often be used without charge, a cooler that held soda (since no alcohol was served) and a few benches for spectators.

George Maynard, who farmed from early morning until the afternoon, would often set up pins at the alley in the evening to earn extra money. Maynard recalled that he was put to work if he showed up, and he was paid at the end of every night.

Lanie Coulter, another longtime Saybrook resident, also set pins for ten cents or fifteen cents a string. At the end of the night, pin setters may have made $1.50 and would usually get good tips from league players. Pin setters had to hustle, clear dead wood and set the pins on little spikes that were raised with a foot pedal. Lanie recalled that a ladies' league from Essex played on Sunday afternoons. He said some would roll the ball very slowly, and on occasion, some pin boys would place a block in the pedal that raised the spikes for the pins. That way, when the very slow-rolling ball finally hit the pins, it would just stop, and the pin would not fall over.

When a forcefully thrown ball hit the small duck pins, they flew in many directions. Pin boys crouched in a corner at the end of the alley to avoid the flying lumber. They cleared and set pins and put the ball in the rack to roll it back and then jumped back into their somewhat protective corner. Big pin bowling was only done by the Ponds League, which bowled with big pins on Saturday afternoon. On Saturday night, after the regular league games were over, others would come in to play for money, and the doors would be locked. Like the soda fountain at the Rexall Drug Store or the movie theater, the bowling alley was a place for young people to meet and have a good time.

The Old Saybrook Bowling Alleys changed ownership a few times, and it was modernized. In the 1960s, the place was either burned down or demolished—perhaps both—and was replaced by the Hubba Hubba Restaurant. Today, the old site is a parking lot. At the other end of town, on the Post Road, another bowling alley, with modern equipment, attracted a new generation of bowlers, but it, too, was finally forced to close in the early 2000s. Its building was demolished in 2019, and it was replaced by a gardening supply shop and a coffee and donut establishment. Although bowling was once called the greatest of indoor sports, that title must now be passed to something more electronic—all that's missing is the friendship of fellow human beings.

17

MATINEE ON MAIN

For people of a certain age, movies hold a nostalgic sort of fondness. For this generation, twenty-five cents for admission opened a world of continuous Saturday matinees. There, in the dark with friends, one could watch a double feature, selected short subjects and even the Pathe newsreels of the world. The theater became an exciting weekly attraction that satisfied youthful social life. So, it was a big improvement when the new two-story brick Colonial-style theater, with six hundred seats and a large screen, replaced the movies previously shown by Thomas P. Kerwin at the Saybrook Town Hall.

The country was still deep in the Great Depression when Irving and Leo Bonoff of Madison purchased the land and had a theater constructed for the rather princely sum of $50,000. It was completed in January 1937, with two adjoining shops that were leased by O'Brien's Colonial Shoppe and Connolly's Men Shop. The following year, the Bonoffs were awarded a contract from the U.S. Post Office and built additions on each side of their theater. The post office moved into the new location and remained there until it moved farther up Main Street in 1950. It later moved across the street to its current building, where it has been since the early 1970s.

The theater was a major entertainment source for local residents, and long lines there were a common sight. Local film historian Fred Beebe made his own movies of people going to the movies. Many young couples had their first Saturday night dates at the theater. They may have seen Fred Astaire and Ginger Rogers, Shirley Temple, Clark Gable, Mickey Rooney or Judy

Built in 1937, the theater was designed to seat six hundred people. Alongside it was the post office, Young's Soda Shop and Fred's Beauty Shop. *Image courtesy of Old Saybrook Historical Society.*

Garland. The local favorite, of course, was Hollywood legend and Fenwick resident Katharine Hepburn.

Always popular were the films produced with scenes from local towns, and they often used local people in supporting roles. The film *Parrish* is the story of young Parrish McLean, who lived on a tobacco plantation in Connecticut with his ruthless tobacco tycoon stepfather. Several scenes with Karl Malden and Claudette Colbert were shot at the Terra Mar at Saybrook Point. In the 1970s, a grade B horror film titled *Let's Scare Jessica to Death* filmed several scenes at the Piontkowski family's residence across from the auto mall on Middlesex Turnpike. Nearby, in Chester, Hollywood stars Doris Day, Jack Lemmon and Ernie Kovacs were joined by several dozen local residents in *It Happened to Jane*. The film is frequently re-shown in Chester, and it is always welcomed with enthusiasm.

Throughout the years, the facility served as a place for school entertainment events, fashion shows, magic shows, lectures and even a talk by First Lady Eleanor Roosevelt. In 1967, the building was renovated, but the plans to redesign the popular white-pillared entrance, with its mural of natives watching ships approaching the shore, were abandoned after townspeople objected. Remodeling and name changes were unable to

FRIDAY and SATURDAY, MARCH 4 and 5

It's swingy...
It's zingy...
with the brightest stars of Swing Lane
to entertain you as never before!

52ND STREET

IAN HUNTER · LEO CARRILLO
PAT PATERSON · ELLA LOGAN
SID SILVERS · ZASU PITTS

Shown at 6:30 and 9:30 P. M.

also "SHE LOVED A FIREMAN"
with Dick Foran - Ann Sheridan

"She Loved a Fireman" Shown at 8:20

Added—"AUDIOSCOPIKS"-Third Dimension on the Screen
Play "TEN-O-WIN" — FRIDAY NIGHT

— Coming to this Theatre Soon! —

A Picture Too Beautiful To Describe.

SNOW WHITE
AND THE SEVEN DWARFS

WALT DISNEY'S
First Full Length Feature
in TECHNICOLOR

Left: Hollywood films grew increasingly popular during the 1940s, with the young and old regularly attending Saturday performances. Among the memorable films were Walt Disney's feature cartoons. *Image courtesy of Old Saybrook Historical Society.*

Below: An idyllic scene of a boy and his dog at "Saybrook Landing" can be seen today at the old movie theater. *Image courtesy of Sally Perrenten.*

save the theater. The film industry, distribution arrangements and movie tastes were all changing. Ticket sales were slipping. A new six-screen cinema opened in nearby Porter Plaza, and the old theater screened its last film on February 27, 2000.

The theater's new owners renovated it and reopened the building for commercial shops in 2004. The old mural was removed, but it could not survive cleaning. Today, in the theater's domed portico, there is an attractive waterfront scene that was painted by muralist Tony Falcone; it shows a boy and his dog at an imaginary Saybrook Landing. The building has been subdivided, and there are second-floor offices, restaurants and retail shops. Other than its classic appearance, the theater's only connection to the movies today is its dance studio in the old post office section that is named after Fred Astaire.

18

KEEPING THE FAITH

*A*s organizations change over time, differences develop among their members, including the members and leaders of religious organizations. Who makes decisions and how they get made were the subjects of a momentous church gathering in Saybrook that prepared a document that came to be known as the Saybrook Platform.

In early colonial days, the Congregational Church was the one and only church, and beginning in 1650, all persons were required to pay taxes to support it and its minister. Town meetings decided community and church matters at the same time. Establishing new churches required the approval of the legislature and of neighboring churches.

When Reverend Gurdon Saltonstall of New London became governor in 1707, he sought to establish stricter church government. Following his leadership, in May 1708, the legislature called for a meeting to consider and agree on methods and rules for the management of church affairs. At this time, there were little more than forty Congregational churches in the colony, with one Baptist church in Groton and one Episcopal church in Stratford, both formed in 1707. Since many of the attending ministers were also trustees of the collegiate school and would be in attendance at the commencement of the graduates, the general assembly directed the delegates to meet in Saybrook. Their instructions were to prepare recommendations for the general court to consider and adopt to provide order in the church system. The meeting began on September 9, 1708.

THIRD MEETINGHOUSE
Congregational

From 1726-1839 the Third Meetinghouse stood
on this Church Green on land generously
given by John Pratt and his son, Isaac.
Measuring 48 feet long by 38 feet wide,
the building's main entrance was located on
the long south side. A tower and spire were
added to the east side in 1793 and a bell in 1794.
The bell "was tolled for weddings, wakes
and the minister as he was seen approaching."
The only heat was supplied by individual
foot stoves. For these 113 years three ministers—
Frederick W. Hotchkiss, William Hart and
Azariah Mather ably served the members.

Erected by the
First Church of Christ in Saybrook
(Congregational)
2007

The Congregational church in
Old Saybrook was established at
Saybrook Fort in 1646. *Image courtesy
of Old Saybrook Historical Society.*

There were sixteen members, twelve of whom were ministers and four of whom were laymen, and two of those members came from the Saybrook church, Robert Chapman and Deacon William Parker. Reverend Thomas Buckingham of Saybrook, who privately studied theology and began preaching in Wethersfield when he was eighteen, and Reverend James Noyes of Stonington were the moderators of the body. All of the clergy, with the exception of Reverend Buckingham, were graduates of Harvard. The group either met in Reverend Buckingham's house or that of Nathaniel Lynde, who had previously given it to the collegiate school. Other meetings were likely held in the Saybrook Congregational church, which was built in 1681 on Middle Lane, facing the green, across from the old burying ground. There are no records of their deliberations, but many believe that Reverend James Pierpont of New Haven wrote the original draft of the platform.

The following October, the platform was unanimously adopted and sent to the legislature, which adopted it with the stipulation—in order to appease those who disagreed with the results—that nothing shall hinder or prevent those "who soberly differ or dissent from the united churches hereby established, from exercising worship and discipline, in their own way, according to their consciences." In 1710, Thomas Short of New London printed *The Saybrook Platform of Church Discipline.* It was the first book printed in the Connecticut Colony.

The heart of the platform is found in its articles of church discipline. Designed "for the better regulation of the administration of church discipline," it provides for county "consociations" to enforce discipline and doctrine in the churches, a ministerial association to regulate ordinations and a general association of ministers to oversee church affairs in the colony. All of these were important, but controversial, steps. Some thought the articles infringed on the independence of the individual churches. Others felt they did not go far enough in making changes and reinforced the views of the conservative churches. Although many churches in

The fourth church building was dedicated in 1840. It was extensively renovated in 1977 and remains in use today. *Image courtesy of Old Saybrook Historical Society.*

Fairfield County thought they were too liberal, many modern historians see it as a conservative attempt to hold onto power.

However, the Saybrook Platform provided mutual aid and assistance in handling church disputes. Some credit the platform with allowing Congregationalists to maintain their independent religious integrity that enabled their contributions during the American Revolution, their religious revivals, their opposition to slavery and their call to missions that would take the faith westward and around the world. The Saybrook Platform remained state law until 1784. By 1791, the state legislature granted the right of free incorporation to all religious bodies, but persons not associated with any church were still required to pay taxes to the established Congregational church. This was not changed until the state's new constitution of 1818 made all contributions voluntary.

Today, the Congregational Church structure retains consociations and associations that meet regularly to discuss church affairs and advise local churches. But, in the words of today's United Church of Christ constitution, the "autonomy of the local church is inherent and modifiable only by its own action."

19

PLANTING SEEDS

Statements about planting seeds are typically used as a way to note small beginnings that eventually bear fruit. So, when Reverend Peter G. Clarke of Essex traveled south, to Saybrook, in August 1825 to hold Episcopal services for twelve congregants in a private residence and, later, in the Center Schoolhouse, he was planting the kernels of a religious faith that had modest beginnings elsewhere in Connecticut.

Episcopal services in Connecticut were probably first held in Stratford, and a minister was appointed there in 1713. By the end of the American Revolution, there were forty-four parishes in the new state. Although Samuel Seabury (1729–1796) was an unwavering Loyalist during the Revolution and an author of three letters written under the penname A.W. Farmer condemning the Continental Congress, he became the first bishop of Connecticut on November 14, 1784. His early appointment made Connecticut the oldest diocese in the Episcopal Church. In Saybrook, Grace Episcopal Church is the oldest and only early nineteenth-century non-Congregational church that remains in existence.

After holding services in the Center Schoolhouse for five years, the growing congregation was ready for a larger and more traditional house of worship. In May 1830, it voted to organize under the name of Grace Church and build its own structure. The organizers included several pillars of the Saybrook community: Richard Hart, William Lynde, Richard Chalker, Richard Pratt, Augustus Chalker, William Willard, Ira Bushnell and William Clark. Major Richard Hart and his wife donated land on the west side of Main Street, north of their residence, on the corner of the Old Boston Post Road, and Richard and Augustus Chalker did the construction work. The new building was completed under the leadership of Reverend Ashbel Steele, the first rector.

The little white wooden church served its purpose for many years, but by the early 1870s, the congregation desired a larger and improved place of worship. The property was sold to Mrs. Eliza Morgan, and the building was sold to James H. Day and Daniel C. Spencer, who moved it next to the store they owned. The church building remains there today, on the Old Boston Post Road. At its new location, the little church was converted into stores, and over time, it was home to J.A. Ayer's Boot Store, the post office and a meeting hall. In recent times, it has housed Dance Dynamics and two apartments.

The new and present English Gothic–style church was designed by Reverend Jesse Heald. The stone came from the town quarry, which is now the site of the Staples office store on the Boston Post Road. Construction was completed and a cornerstone of Portland brownstone was laid in 1871. The building, which is an architectural attraction today, was consecrated by Reverend John Williams on October 24, 1872. There were 130 communicants. Reverend Heald also provided the design for the rectory, which is said to be a copy of a rectory in England. The original rectory was probably lost to fire and replaced by the present rectory in the early 1890s.

For years, the Hart family was a major contributor to Grace Church. Major Richard and Elizabeth Hart contributed land for the building and a pipe organ, the first of its kind in the area. A large stained-glass window over the entrance was given in their memory. Elisha Hart provided lamps for the pulpit. Mr. and Mrs. Samuel Hart donated the communion table and lamps. Bibles and prayer books were a gift from Mrs. Richard Hart. Reverend Samuel Hart (1845–1917), also called Dr. Hart, contributed his scholarly wisdom to the church. Born in Saybrook and baptized at Grace Church, Hart attended Trinity College and then stayed there to become a professor in mathematics and Latin. Highly respected, he held several prestigious positions within the local Episcopal church, including secretary to the house of bishops, historiographer of the church and dean of the Berkeley Divinity School.

A parish house was built by the Grace Church Guild, an organization that was formed in 1895 by the women of the church. When the building was completed in 1897, the group was disbanded. The parish house itself

Left: The first Episcopal service was held in Saybrook in 1825. *Image courtesy of Old Saybrook Historical Society.*

Below: Grace Episcopal Church was built in 1873 with material from the public stone pits near the Oyster River Highway. *Image courtesy of Old Saybrook Historical Society.*

remained until a new one was constructed in 1967. The new parish house was named for Reverend Edward R. Merrill, who served as rector from 1948 to 1969. Immediately north of the church is the Chapman House, which was purchased in 1972 to serve as office and meeting space, but in recent years, it has been used as a residence.

In addition to the architectural beauty of the church and the rectory, perhaps the most eye-catching structure on the property is the church's massive pale pink granite sign. This two-ton, two-by-two-by-seven-foot block of granite was a gift of parishioner Gerry Drechsler, who found the stone in Clinton. Originally in the foundation of the Amtrak bridge over Clinton's Liberty Street, the stone came from the Stony Creek quarry. It was cleaned and sandblasted by Becker Granite Company of Middletown, which also engraved the church's name in the stone and tinted the letters a dark color for visibility. It was installed on October 1, 1997.

Since those early seed-planting days, Grace Church has flourished as a center of the community. Its wide-ranging efforts span the globe, from scholarships in Africa to raising funds for Saybrook's Youth and Family Services, assisting those trying to overcome alcohol addiction and sponsoring a Boy Scout troop. The church also sponsors a Wednesday food site, which collects canned goods and staple items, and conducts a heat-'n-eat program. The site has volunteers, along with members of the community, who maintain a half-acre "Common Good" garden behind the church, where they plant, care for and harvest garden produce that is delivered to several local food pantries. They are planting seeds for improving lives.

20

FROM FACTORY TO MAIN STREET

*E*arly French and Spanish explorers of the Americas were Catholic, but it was not until the large influx of Irish immigrants in the mid-1800s that a sizeable number of Catholics arrived in the United States. The few Catholics in Connecticut had limited rights, as did other religious groups, until a new state constitution was ratified in 1818. It was not until 1829 that the first Catholic church was established in Hartford, and it was followed in 1833 by a church in New Haven and by another in Bridgeport in 1843. With the increasing number of Irish immigrants, an energetic and ignorant number of citizens calling themselves the American Party—or, more commonly, the Know-Nothings—opposed foreigners and Catholics and were politically powerful for several years.

By 1850, the Diocese of Hartford had twelve Catholic churches, fourteen priests and a population of twenty thousand parishioners. With a flood of newly arrived immigrants, membership doubled the following year to forty thousand members of the church. By the mid-nineteenth century, Reverend John Brady of Hartford visited Chester, with its ten families and forty persons professing the Catholic faith, to consider organizing a parish. For the next quarter century, visiting priests from other parishes came to celebrate mass in private homes.

The few Catholics in Saybrook were under the jurisdiction of Father Lynch of Chester until he moved to Guilford in 1856. Masses were conducted by priests visiting from Branford, Chester and New London, and they were held in private homes before they were moved to the Academy on Main Street in Old Saybrook. With a small but growing Catholic population, Saybrook's members of the church looked to obtain their own house of worship. Their opportunity came when an empty and neglected building on two acres, which was originally constructed in 1854 alongside the railroad tracks to manufacture skates, became available. Arrangements to purchase the land may have been made by Reverend Thomas Quinn in 1864, but it was not until September 1869 that an actual purchase was made. Saybrook town records show that the church bought two acres from Francis McFarland of Providence, Rhode Island, "near the station house of the New Haven and New London Railroad."

Located on Old Middlesex Turnpike, the main highway into town from the north, the original church was situated near the front entrance of today's cemetery. When the railroad constructed a bridge over the tracks on Route 1 in the 1920s, that became the main road for automobile traffic. Today, large barriers prevent traffic from crossing the railroad tracks to travel on the old turnpike. Many of today's railroad passengers waiting for the train west, to New Haven or New York, can easily view the cemetery alongside the tracks.

It was started in the mid-1860s and rededicated in 1940, when twin brick entrance columns were erected to hold the sign identifying it as "St. John's R.C. Cemetery." The first burials curiously recorded on gravestones, before the church building was acquired in 1869, were those of six-week-old Daniel Osborn and soldier Patrick O'Brien, who served in Company F, Seventy-First Regiment New York Infantry during the Civil War. Both were buried in 1865. The next burial, which did not occur until October 1867, was that of John Nagle, another Civil War veteran, who served with Company C, Fourteenth Regiment New York Infantry. According to Don Sparaco, the longtime and, now, retired caretaker of the cemetery's two acres and more than two hundred gravesites, the property was overgrown and neglected when Reverend Eugene Salega, who served from 1969 to 1985, asked if he could bring it back. Sparaco said that all of the earlier burial records were destroyed or lost when the church rectory was flooded. While the cemetery is considered closed, some families have plots, which they can use, and there are a few burials each year in these family plots. With no records or maps, locating these plots is often a cautious undertaking.

After the early purchase of the old skate factory, the building was renovated and converted into a church with pews, stained-glass windows, an organ and a steeple. Masses were held there starting in 1875, and the following year, it was incorporated as a mission church. Then, on October 26, 1884, a dedication ceremony with a bishop's mass officially named the church St.

John the Evangelist. Additional land was purchased in the 1880s and, again, in 1911 to provide additional space for the cemetery. By 1900, there were nearly two hundred members of the church, and the Catholic population of Old Saybrook was increasing, especially with the addition of summer residents. A larger facility was needed.

Reverend Martin O'Brien, the church's first resident pastor, planned for a larger church and acquired three properties, totaling fourteen acres, on Main Street in 1914 and 1920. When Father O'Brien was promoted to the pastorate of Seymour, he was replaced by Reverend James Hussion in 1919. Additional land, including the Ely House and the Elisha Hart House on Main Street, was purchased in 1921. Efforts led by Father Hussion culminated in the completion of a new gray brick church designed in an English Gothic architectural style. In ceremonies attended by many church dignitaries, the church was dedicated by Bishop John H. Nilan, and a cornerstone was laid by Father Hussion on July 6, 1930. The interior is paneled in oak, with marble altars, and a large organ occupies the front part of the structure. The old church on North Main Street was demolished in 1930. The pews and salvageable church objects were sent to the church in Moodus.

Old Saybrook's parish continued to grow, and in the early 1960s, construction began on a school. Opened in 1964, with seventy students

Residents attempted to manufacture skates in the 1850s but were unsuccessful. They sold their building, and it was converted into a Catholic church. *Image courtesy of Old Saybrook Historical Society.*

The Saybrook parish was established in the 1880s as a mission of the church in Chester, and it became a separate parish in 1914. *Image courtesy of Old Saybrook Historical Society.*

in grades one and two, a grade was added each year, and the first eighth grade class graduated in 1972. But that success was accompanied by financial difficulties and the withdrawal of the sisters who staffed the school. With no replacements, the school closed and served as a parish center, housing the religious education office. The school reopened with eighty-two students from pre-kindergarten to eighth grade in 1994, and it was staffed by the Sisters of Charity of Our Lady. It was the only Catholic school to open in the United States that year. The student enrollment grew; additions were needed in the late 1990s, and several improvements were made in the early 2000s.

St. John is under the jurisdiction of the Diocese of Norwich, which was officially established when it was separated from the Hartford Diocese on August 6, 1953. In recent times, the parish has joined with Westbrook to share facilities and personnel.

21

WHEN WE WERE A COUPLE O' KIDS

School days, school days
Dear old Golden Rule days
Reading and 'riting and 'rithmetic
Taught to the tune of the hick'ry stick
You were my queen in calico
I was your bashful, barefoot beau
And you wrote on my slate, "I Love You, Joe"
When we were a couple o' kids

By Gus Edwards, Will D. Cobb
Published 1907

Myths and faulty memories created a romantic image of the "little red schoolhouse," but they were far from being a beacon of learning; they were shabby, unpainted buildings, with little equipment, a limited curriculum, one untrained and poorly paid teacher and many unruly students of all ages. But for their day, they provided a useable education and promoted democracy. Saybrook had four schoolhouses that were located in districts at Ferry Point, Oyster River, Saybrook Point and in the center of town.

Growing dissatisfaction with these small, isolated, inefficient schools led some residents to begin asking for one large school to handle the entire student population. The proposal created bitter opposition. Some parents objected to sending their children so far away from home. Others said it would depreciate the value of farm property. And then, as now, there were those who thought it would raise taxes and be too costly. As a result, the proposal to combine the district schools was rejected at a town meeting.

Those who favored the new school kept up their efforts, and another town meeting was held on the evening of July 27, 1891. At the meeting, opponents objected to non–property holders voting away the taxpayers' money. In the end, the idea of having a consolidated school passed; $10,000 was appropriated for construction, and a building committee was appointed to receive plans, review estimates and award contracts. Soon after, a building site on Main Street was purchased from Giles A. Bushnell, and a design prepared by well-known New London architect George Warren Cole was accepted. In October 1891, a contract was awarded to Saybrook builder John Tileston, and ground was soon broken for a new school.

The finished structure was a two-story wooden building with a stone foundation. From its concrete floored basement to its ten-foot-tall rounded tower, the school provided an impressive and graceful image for a confident community. The total cost of the fifty-six-by-thirty-one-square-foot building was $9,965, some $35 under budget. A double flight of wooden steps led to a platform and the main entrance. Passing through two heavy plate-glass doors, a visitor would enter a long ten-foot-wide corridor lined with yellow pine. The second-floor corridor was the same, although the walls were studded with numbered hooks for each student's apparel. The basement was large and well-lit, and it contained the boiler room and a huge coal bin, which supplied a large hot water heater that warmed the building.

The school opened on September 12, 1892, with Principal F.A. Curtis, 5 teachers and approximately 210 students. The school consolidated the district schools and every grade from kindergarten to grade twelve. The rear part of the building was the primary school and had eight classrooms. The front of the building was the high school. Supporters quickly noted an increased interest in "books and the general acquiring of knowledge." They praised the management of the school and its excellent educational facilities. Even the school's bitterest opponents, according to the local newspaper, were forced to admit that its results were beginning to show "a higher intellectual development among [the town's] young men and young women." The newspaper concluded that the old district school had had its day. "At present, a more careful classification and grading of the student according to his or her abilities is needed and called for, and such is supplied in an institution like the present Old Saybrook School."

Left: District schools were closed in 1892 and replaced by the consolidated school in the center of town. *Image courtesy of Old Saybrook Historical Society.*

Below: This building was constructed in 1936, during the Great Depression, and served all students until an increased population required additional buildings. *Image courtesy of Old Saybrook Historical Society.*

The consolidated "wood school" remained until a new "brick school" replaced it in September 1937. In an interview some time ago, Anne Sweet, an accomplished local historian who is now deceased, remembered starting school there in first grade and graduating high school there in 1938. She recalled hating girls' basketball because players had to stop at the center line and could never finish a play. On rainy days, the students played volleyball inside. In her classes, she said that they had a lot of yellow paper and that it was very special to do work on white paper. "All classrooms were quiet. You raised your hand if you had something important to say, and it better be important. They were pleasant times."

Gloria Cahill Fogg, who served as the assistant and then treasurer of the Town of Old Saybrook from 1969 to 1999, started in the consolidated school in May 1932. She remembered crossing empty lots to return to her Elm Street farm for lunch. She observed, "Education is important. Take advantage of all opportunities. Today, there are a lot more opportunities than we ever had."

Ruth Nuhn, who started kindergarten in the old wood school, said she remembers being very nervous and apprehensive about going to school. She lived on a farm, and just to travel to Main Street was big deal. But, she said, looking back, she had superb teachers in a marvelous school. She remembered reading the classics in literature, and she went on to the women's division of the University of Virginia, where she eventually became a reading specialist.

Moving from a small, poorly equipped district school, with a single teacher and students of many ages, to a graded system, with trained teachers, enriched curriculum, special instruction, advanced equipment and skilled supervision, was one of the most significant advances in public education. The lesson for today may be that it is not the test scores that count, it's whether we provide a useful education and promote democracy. For its day, the old consolidated school succeeded.

22

TEAMMATES START THE FIRE DEPARTMENT

By J. T. Dunn

*A*n enduring friendship between two men that began in a boys' military school was fostered by baseball and their love of Old Saybrook, and it gave birth to the Old Saybrook Fire Department in August 1924.

Probate judge Charles S. Gates (1861–1937) was a well-respected man in town. Often endorsed by both political parties for the position he held for thirty years, despite his lack of formal legal training, he was also a local teacher, a railway clerk at the train station, a chairman of the school board for thirty years and he served on the draft board during World War I.

On April 10, 1924, Judge Gates wrote Finley J. Shepard of New York City, suggesting that, as he had always maintained a kindly feeling for the old town and visited it each summer, he might wish to donate a fire apparatus to meet its needs. This would seem to be an exorbitant request by Judge Gates to a citizen of New York City, but the two were very old friends.

Finley J. Shepard (1867–1942), nicknamed Fin, was born in Old Saybrook, most likely in the Hart House where his father, Reverend Peter L. Shepard, the rector of the Grace Episcopal Church, was an instructor. In the year of Fin's birth, Reverend Shepard purchased the large home and property at 341 Main Street from the Kirtlands. This home and its grounds became a military school for boys called the Seabury Institute. Judge Gates and Finley Shepard both attended school together at the institute named for Bishop Seabury.

In 1881 and 1882, the pair played baseball for Old Saybrook against teams from Westerly, Rhode Island; Stonington; Mystic; Meriden; Chester; Deep River; Plainville; East Hampton; Black Hall; and Middletown. Shepard was the pitcher and Gates was the catcher. Old Saybrook's team was famous in the area for two reasons: its winning record and the fact that the team was made up of boys from the town. Many of the area's teams brought in big leaguers, who were paid for each game and received jobs in the towns that they played for. They did this under the guise of visiting family relatives for the summer. Games were held on weekends and holidays, and each was followed by a banquet.

The coach of the Old Saybrook team was Charley Howard, who lived at the Coulter House (present-day Monkey Farm). The Coulter House was the center for baseball fans following the team. In 1881, the team won eighteen out of their thirty-seven games. In 1882, they were undefeated in their eighteen games. Shepard was well known for being the first pitcher in the area to use a curveball and the sudden drop.

After the winning seasons, at the age of eighteen, Finley Shepard left to travel west, causing the breakup of the team. He first moved to Chicago, working in a bookstore, and later took similar work in St. Paul while living with the family of baseball shortstop Ben Worley. He gained employment in the auditing office of the Northern Pacific Railroad; after two years, he was promoted to assistant general manager. After moving back to Chicago, Fin worked for the Atchison Topeka and Santa Fe Railroad, and within a year, he became the general superintendent of the Pacific Coast Lines. In June 1911, Fin began working for the operating department of the Missouri Pacific Railroad, rising to the position of assistant to the president a year later.

In 1912, Finley Shepard was known as one of the most capable all-around railroad men in the country. The same year, he was engaged to Helen Gould, who was described in a December 1912 *Hartford Courant* article as the "best beloved woman in all of the Americas."

Helen Gould was a famous philanthropist and a daughter of railroad tycoon Jay Gould, who died in 1892, leaving her a significant inheritance. Jay Gould was deeply involved in the Tammany Hall–Boss Tweed corruption scandal of New York City in the 1860s and 1870s. By the 1880s, he owned one-ninth of all rail in the United States, and he had a controlling interest in Western Union Telegraph.

Helen Gould was respected for donating large sums of money to the United States during the Spanish-American War; she later donated money to the government for medical supplies. She traveled the country, donating to YWCA projects and serving on the national board of the YWCA.

Finley Shepard and Helen Gould had known each other for some time. Neither had been married; he was forty-five and she was forty-four. On October 5, 1912, Fin was asked by the president of the railroad to escort Miss Gould from New York to Chicago for a YWCA event. They traveled in a private car at the end of the train. Ahead, a freight train near Buffalo crashed into the train, sending some of the cars over the track. It was a terrible tragedy. The *New York Times* reported that Fin spent more than an hour with an axe and a shovel freeing people, and Miss Gould, with a medicine kit, attended the injured with the calmness of a trained nurse. When the two restarted their trip to Chicago, they were engaged. The engagement was national news, and reporters descended on Old Saybrook to write the story and speak to friends and family.

In April 1924, when Fin received a letter from his old schoolmate and catcher Judge Gates asking him for help with a fire apparatus for Old Saybrook, he promptly agreed to help on the condition that the town act on the offer by June 30. A surprise town meeting was called, but a few, aside from the board of selectmen, knew the purpose. Due to the mystery, the attendance was large.

Finley Shepard donated $4,000.00 toward purchasing an engine. A committee of five chose an American LaFrance, and a parade was held when it arrived that August. Additional funds were approved by the town for housing the engine and equipment: $3,087.00 for the firehouse, $50.56

The first firehouse was a shed behind the town hall; it housed a single truck, an American LaFrance chemical engine. *Photograph courtesy of Old Saybrook Fire Department.*

The Old Saybrook Fire Department was chartered in 1924 as a volunteer service. The first fire chief was Gordon Smith. *Image courtesy of Old Saybrook Historical Society.*

for supplies, $15.00 for insurance and $3.00 for lights. The new firehouse was built behind the old town hall. Mrs. Acton donated $600.00 to buy the necessary fire alarm system for the town.

The first firemen were accepted on August 26, 1924, and they included Gordon B. Smith (later elected the first fire chief), Harry Smith, Fred LaMay, Dr. William Wolfe, Fred Stokes, Herb Stokes, John Coulter, Fitzhugh Dibble and Carl Warren.

Bylaws were drafted and postcards were sent to other men in town that read: "You are invited to become a charter member of the Old Saybrook Fire Department at a meeting to be held in the town hall September 10, 1924, at 8:00 p.m. Non-attendance at this meeting will be considered as your refusal to become a member. Signed—The Committee." Some twenty-nine men accepted the invitation, making the charter members thirty-eight strong.

Since that day in 1924, several hundred men and women have served with the Old Saybrook Fire Department, and today, there is an active and trained volunteer membership. Two firefighters have died in the line of duty: assistant chief Arthur Harrington on March 17, 1947, and firefighter Henry Davis on August 24, 1978.

J.T. Dunn is a former chief of the Old Saybrook Fire Department.

23

SKILLS AND DRILLS
AT SEABURY INSTITUTE

South of the center of Saybrook sits a stately old Italianate house that does not quite fit in with the neighboring Colonials. Its architectural style was popular between the 1840s and 1880s, but its genteel Victorian disguise hides its age and experiences. Just as today's media-savvy youngsters may think a Royal Portable is a monarch's baby, so, too, does the casual passerby misjudge the life of this grand old countess.

Originally built in the 1770s, this home was, for many years, a typical two-story residence. In September 1867, Reverend Peter Shepard (1825–1912) and his wife, the former Mary Anna Burr of Wilmington, North Carolina, purchased the building along with twelve acres from William and Emiline Kirtland. In addition to being the former rector of Grace Episcopal Church, Shepard was an instructor at the school run by Hetty and Nancy Wood, across the street in the General William Hart House. Shepard intended to open his own boarding school, the Seabury Institute, which he named after the first Episcopal bishop in the United States. It was 1865 when he opened the doors, and by the 1868–1869 school year, there were seventy boys and twenty-six girls as day students. He soon added a mansard-style third floor, and behind the main building, he constructed a combined chapel and gymnasium, which is still standing today as a private residence around the corner on the appropriately named Shepard Street.

In his catalogs, Shepard promoted his school and praised the community. The healthful Saybrook environment, he said, is "free from epidemics of all kinds, and temptations and baneful influences incident to city schools." In

Reverend P.O. Shepard, the former rector at Grace Church and a former teacher at the school run by Miss Hetty Wood, opened a school in his home and called it the Seabury Institute. It later provided military training. *Image courtesy of Old Saybrook Historical Society.*

the July 1871 circular, he characteristically reported, "[The town] is one of the most healthful and desirable in the country." The school, he said, is in "a quiet, moral and intelligent community, and remote from the temptations and vice incident to large towns and cities." Ah, the good old days.

The course of study included English, the classics, modern languages, music, drawing and painting. Instruction included frequent reviews and discussions of the subjects. For penmanship, the Spencerian system was taught every day to assist pupils in acquiring "a rapid, graceful and business hand." Each day opened and closed with vocal music, and Mrs. Shepard provided instruction in piano and "the culture of the voice." All students were required to attend morning and evening prayers, and there were also daily Bible lessons given by Reverend Shepard. Attendance at Sunday services was required. Discipline was said to be "mild and parental." However, "cheerful obedience to all right rules of conduct and action [was] insisted upon. Corporeal punishment [was] rarely found to be necessary." But, to be clear, "when a pupil [was] found to be incorrigible, and his influence corrupting, his parents [were] required to remove him."

Students at the school wore a blue broadcloth uniform on Sundays and for parades. At other times, a suit could be worn, and it was requested that clothing be as "plain and serviceable as possible." Pupils paid for the material to make their uniforms, and they were required to bring sheets, pillowcases, overshoes, an umbrella, towels, napkins and rings, forks, spoons and toilet articles. "Books and stationery, if required, will be furnished at New York prices." The cost for tuition and board at the school was $300 per year, and it was paid in equal installments at its opening, Christmas and Easter. There were additional charges of $20 each for Latin, Greek, French, German and drawing. Painting was an additional $40, and lessons and the use of the piano cost $60. Laundry service was provided at a cost of $14 for washing a dozen pieces. A seat in church cost $2, and the use of the library cost $1.

A significant feature of the school was its military drill; in fact, the school was occasionally referred to as a military academy. This drill, "calculated to ensure the erect carriage and manly bearing of boys, is daily conducted by an experienced drill master." Light and convenient cadet muskets were borrowed from the state and given to students to perfect their use and care of arms. In 1870, a special act of the general assembly directed the quartermaster general to deliver to Shepard "thirty cadet muskets or carbines with their accoutrement…for the use of students in the said school of Mr. Shepard…provided, that usual bond be taken for the safe return of same, in good order, when demanded by proper authority."

For the 1870–1871 school year, there were forty-four students, including boys from New York City, Jersey City and as far away as Texas. Most of the major towns in Connecticut were represented, and the fifteen students from Saybrook included sons from old and respected families: the Bushnells, the Chalkers and others, including Reverend Shepard's son, Horace B. Shepard. Horace taught at the institute for a short time before becoming a traveling salesman. According to a report in the July 31, 1883 edition of the *New York Times*, Horace killed his supposed wife and took his own life. In a note to his parents, he announced that he was secretly married, although there was no known ceremony. "We have been happy together in life, but we will be happier in death," he wrote. "Our last wish and request is that we may rest together."

Reverend Peter Shepard ran his Seabury Institute from the mid-1860s until 1886, when he rented the facilities to Warwick P. Jackson for five years and moved to Clinton, where he became rector at the Church of the Holy Advent.

SEABURY INSTITUTE.

SAYBROOK, - - - CT.

MONTHLY REPORT.

For _January_ 187 2

Of M _Gilbert Pratt_

			REMARKS
DAYS ABSENT, - - -	$\frac{1}{1}$	NATURAL PHILOSOPHY,	
" TARDY, - - -	$\frac{1}{0}$	CHEMISTRY, - - -	
MORALS, - - - -	_10_	ASTRONOMY, - - -	
DEPORTMENT IN SCHOOL,	_10_	SCIENCE, - - - -	
" IN GENERAL,	_10_	ARITHMETIC, - - -	_9.7_
NEATNESS, - - - -	_10_	BOOK KEEPING, - -	
INDUSTRY, - - - -	_10_	ALGEBRA, - - -	
BIBLE LESSONS, - -		GEOMETRY, - - -	
ORTHOGRAPHY, - -	_9.6_	SURVEYING, - - -	
DEFINITIONS, - - -		FRENCH LANGUAGE, -	
READING, - - - -	_9.9_	SPANISH " -	
ENGLISH GRAMMAR, -		GERMAN " -	
RHETORIC, - - -		LATIN " -	
LANGUAGE LESSONS,		GREEK " -	
HISTORY, - - - -		DECLAMATION, - -	
GEOGRAPHY, - - -		COMPOSITION, - - -	_9.9_
GEOLOGY, - - - -		PENMANSHIP, - - -	_9.7_
PHYSIOLOGY, - - -		MUSIC, - - - -	
DRAWING, - - - -		MILITARY DRILL, - -	
TELEGRAPHY, - - -		....	

The number 10 denotes unqualified excellence ; 9, 8, &c., excellence in corresponding degrees.

P. L. SHEPARD,
Principal.

This monthly report shows that Gilbert Pratt was a well-behaved and accomplished student. _Image courtesy of Old Saybrook Historical Society._

He then attempted to sell the property in 1892 to Charles F. Dickinson of East Lyme for $3,000, but the deal fell through. The 1890s were a period of considerable social change and international upheaval. With the Spanish-American War of 1898, a large number of Cuban students were sent by their wealthy parents to the Seabury Institute, which was then run by Henry M. Selden. At the time, locals often referred to the school as the Cuban School.

With the end of the war, his own advancing age and his responsibilities with the church in Clinton, Shepard sold the property in April 1900 to Caroline and Henry Selden. When Henry died in 1903, the property reverted to Shepard, and he finally resold it to prominent Saybrook resident Nelson Bowes in 1911 for "one dollar and other valuable considerations." Shepard had already retired from his ministerial duties in Clinton, and in 1908, he was given the honorary title of Rector Emeritus. He died at the age of eighty-seven in Clinton in 1912. He was said to have had a "genial and lovable nature" and to be "a man of stimulating personality, great vigor, zeal and intellectual force."

24

LEAVING A LEGACY

*F*or more than seventy years, Frank Stevenson (1912–1997) carefully tended the lawns and plants, the houses and the people in North Cove. Like the natural objects of his affection, he developed deep roots and thrived as "the keeper of the district and its history." He is *the* Frank Stevenson of the Old Saybrook Historical Society's "Frank Stevenson Archives" at 350 Main Street. Stevenson did not have a life that typically gets recognized with the naming of a building. He was born in Saybrook on February 17, 1912, to George and Jenny Spooner Stevenson, both of whom were completely deaf. As the oldest of eight children, Frank often served as a surrogate parent in communicating with his younger siblings. From a very early age, Stevenson helped his father with gardening and landscaping the estates at Saybrook Point.

He attended local schools but left high school to help with his siblings and augment his family's income. During the Great Depression, he joined the National Forestry Service and became a foreman of a work crew to cut trees and fight the gypsy moth infestation. Frank often visited the Kelsey family in Westbrook, where he met and later married Elsie. With the onset of World War II, he joined the army and was sent to Fort Devens in Ayer, Massachusetts. From there, he went into the army air corps and received technical training for aircraft instrumentation at Tinker Air Base in Oklahoma City. After completing his training, he was shipped out on the *Queen Mary* to an airbase in England, where he taught instrument flying to pilots of the Eighth Division of the army air corps.

By the end of the war, staff sergeant Frank Stevenson had received four Bronze Star medals, and his first son, Edward Andrew, had been born. He toured England on a bicycle, which he purchased with money sent by Elsie and other family members. After returning to Old Saybrook, he joined American Legion Post 113, where he remained a member for the rest of his life and served as commander in 1951 and 1952. He was hired by Chapman Fuel Company to drive a truck where he delivered ice, coal and oil and took on a variety of other tasks during the forty years he worked for Howard Chapman. In his spare time, he maintained the properties for the homeowners of North Cove, a task that became full time after he retired from Chapman Fuel.

Bill Phillips was the owner of one of those properties and a native of Chicago. He was a graduate of Cornell and a U.S. Navy officer during the Korean conflict. In 1981, Phillips became the chief executive officer of the large Ogilvy & Mather advertising agency, and with his wife, Barbara Smith, he purchased a home in North Cove. Bill and Barbara routinely spent their working days in New York City or traveling, and they retreated to North Cove when they could. The couple needed a competent, reliable and trustworthy person to care for their place in Old Saybrook. They met Stevenson and arranged to have him care for the house. They recalled that he loved his job and thought of his customers as family. The Phillipses were happy to turn over to him the responsibility of caring for their home.

Stevenson had a rugged, stocky look; his face was a bit marred from cancer operations. He usually wore a cap. He had a dry, quiet sense of humor and a knack for getting along with others. He was confident enough to work on his own terms, and he was caring enough that he valued long-term relationships. Everyone knew his pickup truck, with its passenger side filled with tools and "bargains" making it unusable for human occupation.

Stevenson, the jack-of-all-trades, and Bill Phillips, the master of one, became close friends. There were many times when Stevenson just stopped by to talk. He was self-taught, interested in native artifacts, collected stamps and always had horticultural books, many by Old Lyme naturalist Roger Tory Peterson, and of course, he was interested in North Cove and Saybrook history. Stevenson could also be set in his ways, especially if anyone irritated or upset him. A story is often told of Stevenson visiting a new homeowner and explaining his services and charges for his work. After chatting with the woman for a while, Stevenson began to leave when she called to him: "Now, Frank, what is your best price?" Not a good question. Stevenson didn't answer and kept on walking. He never did any work at that house.

Some years later, aware of Stevenson's declining health, Bill Phillips arranged an eighty-fifth birthday party for February 17, 1997, at the General William Hart House. Phillips had to get Stevenson's son Tom to get him there. Historical Society president Donald Swan said, "It's a miracle we got him here." Swan was joined by several other society presidents who said Stevenson was a "walking encyclopedia of town history" and presented him with a birthday cake decorated with an American flag. First Selectman Laurence Reney read a proclamation from a grateful town that stated Frank was "the keeper of the district and its history." He noted that North Cove was "Frank's District" long before it was officially recognized as a National Historic District.

Stevenson didn't relish the limelight and was teary eyed when receiving congratulations from his many friends. He admitted to being surprised. As Stevenson was not feeling well, his son Tom took him from the celebration to Dr. Franklin on Main Street. From there, he was rushed to Middletown Hospital, where he was operated on for renal problems. He barely regained consciousness before he died less than two weeks later, on March 1, 1997. His son Tom Stevenson served for many years with the local police department and, now that he's retired, is active in the historical society and in local government affairs.

When Edie Gengras called on Bill Phillips for a donation toward the archives building fund, Bill offered to contribute $100,000 if the society and the Saybrook Colony Founders Association could raise $50,000 and if the

Frank Stevenson Archives is a repository of Old Saybrook's historic resources and serves as a center of history. *Image courtesy of Old Saybrook Historical Society.*

These early supporters gave their time, talents and treasure to the historical society. *Front row, left to right*: Anne Sweet, Margaret Bock and Martha Soper. *Back row, left to right*: Elaine Staplins, William Phillips and Polly Timken. *Image courtesy of Old Saybrook Historical Society.*

archives could be named for Frank Stevenson. The funds were raised and the name approved.

The *Hartford Courant* quoted Phillips as saying, "Frank Stevenson [had] an alert questioning manner that tolerated no fools, respected the environment, and he has given much more to the town than he asked in return." Stevenson was a gardener and a caretaker, a counselor and a confidant, a handyman and historian, a truck driver, a World War II navy veteran, a naturalist and an honorable old-time Yankee character. Having the archives named for a man who held no public office but served the public good provides added value for a building that enhances the quality of life in Old Saybrook—a lasting legacy.

25

THE HART OF THE TOWN

*W*hen it comes to summarizing a life on a tombstone, some simply provide the name and birth and death dates of the individual buried there. Other markers, perhaps those that represent those of greater wealth, display accomplishments, a sense of self and may provide more of a life story. That certainly is the case with Saybrook's highest-ranking Revolutionary War soldier and one of its wealthiest and most distinguished residents, William Hart (1746–1817). "In youth active and enterprising," his deteriorating marker at Cypress Cemetery still reads, "he early entered on mercantile and commercial pursuits and sustained a character of unquestioned integrity and extensive respectability. By his talents he rose to some of the first civil and military honors of this state and commanded unusual influence at home and abroad."

The Hart family first arrived in the New World and settled in Massachusetts before moving with Reverend Thomas Hooker to become one of the original proprietors of Hartford in 1635. William Hart was the oldest son of Reverend William and Mary Blague Hart. He had, in the words of an earlier writer, a commanding presence. With "a handsome, manly face and keen, dark eyes, he was born for leadership." He married Esther Buckingham, the granddaughter of Reverend Thomas Buckingham of Yale College and Saybrook Platform fame. In 1767, he built a home on Main Street that currently serves as the headquarters of the Old Saybrook Historical Society.

This painting, created by artist Marek Sarba from a miniature portrait, is based on the only known representation of General William Hart. *Image courtesy of Old Saybrook Historical Society.*

As a young man, Hart managed his family's investments and joined the local militia, where he rose to the rank of captain by 1774. When revolution swept across the land in 1775, he was given the rank of major and put in command of the First Regiment of Light Horse Cavalry. His first call to action was in response to Washington's need for reinforcements against a British attack along the Hudson. Saybrook resident Samuel Tully noted in his diary: "April 9, 1776. General Washington passed through town....July 7, 1776: Troops this day under command of Majr. Hart m'ch'd for New York." The following spring, Major Hart and his cavalry helped defend Danbury against a raid by British General Tyron. Then, in October 1777, he moved his troops to reinforce General Israel Putnam at Fishkill, New York. Observers later described his service as substantial and "unblemished but undistinguished." They concluded, "He was no doubt plagued by a chronic dearth of horses, short rations, lack of uniforms and inadequate ordnance, and he took great pride in his brethren when it was all over, satisfied that republican principles had been justly vindicated and the nation's course securely established."

During the war, Hart's younger brother Elisha, who was later the father of seven beautiful daughters, armed the family's vessels to attack English boats. With a mix of patriotism, adventure and anticipation of substantial reward, these privateers attacked British shipping vessels. Half of what they captured went to Connecticut, and the other half was divided among the ship's owners and crew. With four of the eleven ships outfitted in Saybrook at that time, the Hart family, led by Elisha, attacked British ships along the East Coast, Bermuda and the Caribbean. Their ships included the *Restoration*, which had a single gun and fifteen men, and the *Retaliation*, which had ten guns and fifty men. Although captains and crews were repeatedly captured and exchanged and their ships were forced to remain in port, several cargoes were taken for considerable profit.

After the war, William Hart was appointed major general of the Second Division of Militia for the state. This was the highest rank he held, and local residents, then and now, referred to him as General Hart, a title that carried over into his public activities.

The Hart family had substantial real estate holdings, engaged in shipping and trade and owned two local stores. After the Revolution, Connecticut was granted large tracts of land in today's Ohio. Known as the Firelands, or the Western Reserve, this land was meant to compensate the state for the losses it suffered when the British burned several towns during the war. When Connecticut relinquished its claim to this 120-mile strip of over three million acres south of Lake Erie in 1796, the land was sold to a group of fifty-seven speculators for $1.2 million. Organized as the Connecticut Land Company and headed by Oliver Phelps, a Hartford banker, this group of fifty-seven wealthy speculators included William Hart. The company sent Moses Cleaveland, a Canterbury, Connecticut attorney, to survey the land and get it ready to sell to settlers. Eventually, Connecticut settlers moved into Ohio and established towns with Connecticut names, and William Hart's initial investment of $30,462 proved to be a very profitable one for him and his heirs.

Another revolution of sorts occurred in 1800, when Thomas Jefferson defeated Federalist candidates to win the presidency. Jefferson's supporters, including General Hart, met in New Haven to form a new party. They began printing two newspapers, the *American Mercury* in Hartford and the *New London Bee*, and they urged that the 1662 Royal Charter be replaced with a new constitution for Connecticut and that the Congregational Church be separated from the government. The new Democratic-Republicans, as Jefferson's party was called, nominated General Hart to run for Congress, and over the next several years, they nominated him to run for lieutenant governor and governor. He was never successful and died in 1817, a year before Connecticut approved a new constitution to replace the old Royal Charter, disestablishing the church from the state.

General Hart's house was left to his son Richard, who sold the property to his stepmother and William Hart's second wife, Lucy Buckingham Hart. After her remarriage in 1829, the house changed hands, and some of the land was purchased by the Congregational church, which, in 1840, erected the church that is next door to the Hart House and still used. Eventually, the home came into the possession of Hetty and Nancy Wood, who ran a boarding school for girls in the house. Hetty's nephew, George Berrian, inherited the house. Ownership of the home transferred over the years to Ford and Miriam Walker, Henry deWolf deMauriac and the Congregational Church before it was purchased for $78,000 in 1974 by the Old Saybrook Historical Society.

The well-maintained campus provides an attractive setting for a variety of programs, including this concert by the U.S. Coast Guard Dixieland Jazz Band. *Image courtesy of Old Saybrook Historical Society.*

The fading statement on General Hart's tomb concludes that he was "a pillar to society; and has left a memory respected by his friends, instructive to his family, and honorable to the place in which he lived." His life and times, like others in Saybrook, serve as reminders that the past is always present.

BIBLIOGRAPHY

Chapman, Edward M. *The First Church of Christ in Saybrook*. New Haven, CT: Privately printed under the direction of Yale University Press, 1947.

Cheesebrough, Harriet Chapman. *Glimpses of Saybrook in Colonial Days*. Reprint, Old Saybrook, CT: Celebration 3½ to Commemorate the 350th Anniversary of Saybrook Colony in 1985, 1984.

The Faces and Places of Old Saybrook: A Historical Album. Old Saybrook, CT: Old Saybrook Historical Society, 1985.

Gates, Gilman C. *Saybrook at the Mouth of the Connecticut River*. Orange and New Haven, CT: Press of the Wilson H. Lee Co., 1935.

Grant, Marion Hepburn. *The Hart Dynasty of Saybrook*. West Hartford, CT: Fenwick Production, 1981.

Johnson, Curtis S., publisher. *Three Quarters of a Century: The Life and Times in the Lower Connecticut Valley, as Chronicled for Seventy-Five Years by The New Era*. N.p: Privately printed by the New Era, 1949. Reprinted in 1991.

Levy, Tedd. *The Remarkable Women of Old Saybrook*. Charleston, SC: The History Press, 2013.

Maynard, Barbara J., and Tedd Levy. *Old Saybrook: Postcard History Series*. Charleston, SC: Arcadia Publishing, 2010.

Saybrook's Quadrimillennial. *Commemoration of the 250th Anniversary of the Settlement of Saybrook*. Hartford, CT: Press of Clark & Smith, 1886.

Thompson, Gregory Evan, ed. *Articles of the Saybrook History Buffs*. Old Saybrook, CT: Old Saybrook Historical Society, 2016.

Tully, William. "History of Saybrook." In *The History of Middlesex County, 1635–1885*. New York: J.H. Beers & Co., 1884.

BIBLIOGRAPHY

Selected Websites

Connecticut Main Street Center. www.ctmainstreet.org.
Connecticut State Library. www.ctstatelibrary.org.
Main Street America. www.mainstreet.org.
Old Saybrook Historical Society. www.saybrookhistory.org.
Town of Old Saybrook. www.oldsaybrookct.gov.

ABOUT THE AUTHOR

*T*edd Levy is a former educator who now devotes much of his time to writing about local history. He authored or coauthored *Old Saybrook Postcard History* (Arcadia Publishing, 2010), *The Remarkable Women of Old Saybrook* (The History Press, 2013) and the two-volume *Lessons That Work: Ideas and Activities for Teaching U.S. History*. He has written numerous articles for professional and general circulation publications on history, education and public affairs. He is a former president of the National and Connecticut Councils for the Social Studies, the cofounder of Connecticut History Day and an overseer at Old Sturbridge Village.

Visit us at
www.historypress.com